A WORLD BANK COUNTRY STUDY

Bosnia and Herzegovina

Toward Economic Recovery

Prepared by the World Bank, the European Commission, and the European Bank for Reconstruction and Development

The World Bank
Washington, D.C.

Copyright © 1996
The International Bank for Reconstruction
and Development/ THE WORLD BANK
1818 H Street, N.W.
Washington, D.C. 20433, U.S.A.

All rights reserved
Manufactured in the United States of America
First printing June 1996

World Bank Country Studies are among the many reports originally prepared for internal use as part of the continuing analysis by the Bank of the economic and related conditions of its developing member countries and of its dialogues with the governments. Some of the reports are published in this series with the least possible delay for the use of governments and the academic, business and financial, and development communities. The typescript of this paper therefore has not been prepared in accordance with the procedures appropriate to formal printed texts, and the World Bank accepts no responsibility for errors. Some sources cited in this paper may be informal documents that are not readily available.

The World Bank does not guarantee the accuracy of the data included in this publication and accepts no responsibility whatsoever for any consequence of their use. The boundaries, colors, denominations, and other information shown on any map in this volume do not imply on the part of the World Bank Group any judgment on the legal status of any territory or the endorsement or acceptance of such boundaries.

The material in this publication is copyrighted. Requests for permission to reproduce portions of it should be sent to the Office of the Publisher at the address shown in the copyright notice above. The World Bank encourages dissemination of its work and will normally give permission promptly and, when the reproduction is for noncommercial purposes, without asking a fee. Permission to copy portions for classroom use is granted through the Copyright Clearance Center, Inc., Suite 910, 222 Rosewood Drive, Danvers, Massachusetts 01923, U.S.A.

The complete backlist of publications from the World Bank is shown in the annual *Index of Publications*, which contains an alphabetical title list (with full ordering information) and indexes of subjects, authors, and countries and regions. The latest edition is available free of charge from the Distribution Unit, Office of the Publisher, The World Bank, 1818 H Street, N.W., Washington, D.C. 20433, U.S.A., or from Publications, The World Bank, 66, avenue d'Iéna, 75116 Paris, France.

ISSN: 0253-2123

CONTENTS

List of Boxes

List of Tables

Preface

This volume was prepared in February/March 1996 as a background document of the second donors meeting in support of Bosnia and Herzegovina, held in Burssels on April 12-13, 1996. It contains an analysis of the economic policies and institutional challenges facing the peace makers in Bosnia and the international community.

Despite all the difficulties, including the need to clarify responsibilities, to build transparent and reliable channels for the international aid effort and the need in Bosnia to work simultaneously on reconstruction, reconciliation and transition towards the market economy, a good start has been made in the four months following the signing of the peace agreement. Projects have been designed and negotiated, compromises have been reached between the various levels of governments so that responsibility and accountability could be clarified, and terribly difficult decisions on what are the highest priorities are beginning to be made. Reconstruction in all its dimensions has never happened overnight and cannot be achieved in a matter of only weeks or months in Bosnia. It took years after other wars, even in the most successful cases. Reconstruction is different from humanitarian aid because it has to be sustainable, it has to generate high economic returns and, of course, it requires resources of a larger order of magnitude. Thanks to strong support from the international community and a great effort by Bosnian policy makers, and despite the differences that they are still trying to overcome, a good start has been made. But it is only a start. This initial work will lead to real reconstruction over the coming months if the parties in Bosnia can reach compromises and make the new institutions function, and if the international community really follows up on the pledges made and strongly coordinates the assistance effort so that it can be targeted strategically at the priorities identified. It is a challenge that can and should be met.

I join the authors in hoping that their work can contribute towards peace and recovery in Bosnia and Herzegovina.

Kemal Derviş
Vice President

Acknowledgements

The report was drafted by a team of Bank staff and consultants led by Wei Ding under the general guidance of Christine Wallich, Acting Director, Central Europe Department, the World Bank. Michel Noël, Chief, Country Operations Division, helped to conceptualize the report and provided invaluable comments on successive drafts. The report is based on discussions with government officials that started in Warsaw in early 1995 and continued in Bosnia and Herzegovina in the context of several missions for general policy discussions, and preparation of the Emergency Recovery and Structural Adjustment Credits over the course of 1995-1996. The Bank team is indebted to the many government officials and experts outside of government who provided invaluable help. Government officials and key ministers and their staff in the State, Federation, and Serb Republic governments to whom special thanks are owed include Zlatko Bars, Enver Backovic, Drago Bilandzija, Petar Bosnic, Berina Selimovic-Mehmedbasic, Despotovic, Enes Gotovusa, Sefika Hafisovic, Zlatko Hurtic, Munevar Imamovic, Faruk Ismailbegovic, Izudin Kapetanovic, Mirsad Kikanovic, Novak Kondic, Mladan Loncar, Kasim Omicevic, Obrad Piljak, Jadranko Prlic, Slavisa Rakovic, Radovan Skolko, Bozo Ljubic and Neven Tomic. The Bank staff and consultants include Sebnem Akkaya, Emily Andrews, Michael Borish, Milan Cvikl, William Fox, Egbert Gerken, Ulrich Lachler, Michael Mertaugh, Pedro Rodriguez, Luis Alvaro Sanchez, and Sweder van Wijnbergen. The team would also like to thank the EBRD, and the many staff of the European Commission, in particular Ed Kronenburg, Joly Dixon and Joan Pearce who provided both inputs and advice. The team is also indebted to Scott Brown and others of the IMF for invaluable comments. The photograph on the cover is courtesy of World Vision.

CURRENCY EQUIVALENT

100 Bosnian dinars = 1 Deutsche mark

ACRONYMS AND ABBREVIATIONS

BH	Bosnia and Herzegovina
BHD	Bosnia and Herzegovina dinar
BIS	Bank for International Settlements
DM	Deutsche Mark
EU	European Union
FRY	Federal Republic of Yugoslavia
GDP	Gross domestic product
IBRD	International Bank for Reconstruction and Development
IDA	International Development Association
IFC	International Finance Corporation
IMF	International Monetary Fund
JCC	Joint Civilian Commission
NATO	North Atlantic Treaty Organization
NBBH	National Bank of Bosnia and Herzegovina
OECD	Organization for Economic Co-operation and Development
RPA	Regional Privatization Agencies
SFRY	Socialist Federal Republic of Yugoslavia
UN	United Nations
USSR	Union of Soviet Socialist Republics

Fiscal Year

January 1 - December 31

Introduction

Three months after the signing of the Dayton and Paris accords, the beginnings of normal life are stirring in Bosnia, and economic recovery is beginning. Compliance with the military aspects of the accords has been good. Despite initial difficulties and inclement winter conditions, NATO's Implementation Forces were deployed on the ground. The withdrawal of the three parties' forces behind a zone of separation took place close to schedule, as did the removal of heavy weapons. Most prisoners have been exchanged and the demobilization of soldiers is under way.

Progress has been slower on the civilian side. This is to be expected given the complexity of the tasks to be achieved: the organization of free and fair elections, protection of human rights, establishment of a fair and effective police force, building of democratic and pluralistic institutions, return of displaced persons and refugees, and provision of humanitarian and reconstruction assistance.

However, much more progress is needed, particularly on job creation, economic integration and institution building. A working Federation has yet to be set up, and there is still a lack of confidence—even now, twenty-four months after the Washington agreements of March 1994—between the two Federation partners. While there is either a Bosniac or Bosnian Croat minister and deputy minister in every ministry, teamwork is still wanting, and in effect they still report to separate constituencies. There is even greater lack of trust among the three parties—the State and two Entities within Bosnia and Herzegovina—and the rapprochement with the Serb Republic has been slow.

Full reintegration of all parties, as well as closer integration within the Federation, will likely be a lengthy process. The reasons for slow progress on the civilian side are complex and interlinked. For example, the ability of refugees to return to their homes is intertwined with the ongoing work of the war crimes tribunal. The difficulties to date in establishing a Federal Customs Administration—the linchpin of a Federation budget—relate to, among other things, the failure to integrate the federal police and, more fundamentally, to share power *within* the Federation, and between the Federation and the State. The difficulties encountered in reaching agreement on the joint provision of utilities such as water and power, or on the reintegration of road and rail networks reflect a similar lack of trust at the local and Entity levels. Perhaps, given how recent, bitter, and destructive the war has been, more progress could not have been expected.

What *is* certain is that a strong reconstruction effort that quickly rebuilds Bosnia's economic capacities is critical for peace. Only economic progress that visibly improves peoples' lives will demonstrate that peace and reintegration bring more benefits than war. Fundamental to economic recovery and to peace will be the creation of employment opportunities for those who have been without jobs and hope during the war. Such a reconstruction effort will however require a strong, concerted effort on the part of the international donor community.

Even *with* strong international support, the process of reintegration will not be easy, and the international community must be aware of the difficulties and risks that lie ahead. As the recent experience of the West Bank and Gaza shows, there will be ups and downs in the peace process. To expect otherwise in Bosnia would be unrealistic. Still, there is no realistic alternative to active donor support. Without a concerted donor effort there can be no hope for reconstruction, economic recovery, or reconciliation. Without a durable peace, Bosnia will remain troubled and potentially unstable, and blight the prospects for a peaceful future and economic progress for all countries in the Balkan region.

The World Bank, in cooperation with the European Union and other multilateral and bilateral agencies, began its work on Bosnia and Herzegovina in the spring of 1995, when it initiated discussions with the Republic of Bosnia and Herzegovina and the Federation of Bosnia and Herzegovina on a range of economic policy issues, including the needs for reconstruction of war damages, institution building, and economic reforms. Discussions followed, later, with the Serb Republic. Two reports were prepared, *"Bosnia and Herzegovina: Priorities for Recovery and Growth,"* and *"Bosnia and Herzegovina: Priorities for Recovery and Growth—Sectoral Annexes,"* and presented to the First Donors Conference, held in Brussels in December 1995 and chaired jointly by the World Bank and the European Union.

Since then the Bank and the EU have opened field offices in Sarajevo and started to provide concrete financial support to the reconstruction effort on the ground, in close cooperation with other donors. On April 1, the membership of Bosnia and Herzegovina in the World Bank, IDA and IFC was announced, effective February 25, 1993, the date of succession to the membership of the SFRY.

This present report, prepared for the second Donors' Conference jointly sponsored by the European Union and the World Bank in April, 1996, serves two purposes. First, it provides a framework for understanding the challenges facing Bosnia in the critical period ahead as it seeks simultaneously to reconstruct its devastated economy, strengthen economic management, and undertake the transition from socialism to a market economy. Second, it provides background information on the new State and Entity structures that have emerged since the signing of the Dayton and Paris accords; it provides an update on Bosnia's macroeconomic situation, policies, and recent economic performance; and outlines policy options for structural reforms in the public sector and in the enterprise and banking systems. While this report presents a comprehensive view of the challenges facing the Bosnian authorities over the next three years, it also acknowledges the considerable difficulties faced in implementing this agenda, and points to the actions requiring the most urgent attention over the coming months.

A companion volume, "*Bosnia and Herzegovina: The Priority Reconstruction and Recovery Program-The Challenges Ahead*," focuses on sector-by-sector reconstruction needs in the $5.1 billion reconstruction program and policy issues. This volume is available from the Bank upon request (EC2DR).

We and all of those who participated in the preparation of this report hope that our joint efforts can contribute towards peace, justice, and economic recovery that improves the lives of the people of Bosnia and Herzegovina.

Executive Summary

With the advent of peace, there is new hope for the people of Bosnia and Herzegovina, whose long suffering from a devastating war has been transformed into an earnest desire for peace and prosperity. After four years of trauma, poverty, and subsistence living, the people of Bosnia and Herzegovina are hoping for nothing less than a quick and substantial betterment of their lives. In this new environment, economic reconstruction and recovery have become the focal point for both policy makers and the public: the outcome could cement or shatter the ongoing peace process. The challenge is of immense proportions: history shows that it is always difficult to rebuild after a prolonged war. It is doubly difficult to undertake the task when it involves setting up new governance structures and institutions. Undertaking such a task with a socialist legacy and major unresolved structural problems in industry, banking, and economic management—as is the case for Bosnia and Herzegovina—is truly heroic. In this undertaking, Bosnia and Herzegovina faces three major challenges:

- *First, implementing the reconstruction and recovery program necessitated by the war damage.* Bridges, roads, housing, and water and sewerage facilities need to be repaired and public services restored. Hundreds of thousands of refugees and displaced persons need to be resettled and soldiers demobilized. Employment will need to be created in order to reintegrate them into economic life. Economic revival and employment generation will be driven mostly by the reconstruction program in the initial stage of economic recovery in Bosnia. Appropriate organization, coordination, and implementation of the reconstruction program will be key to maximizing its impact on domestic economic recovery and employment generation.

- *Second, developing the new governance structure and institutions for economic management.* Institutions at all levels of government need to be created or consolidated in order to implement the blueprint laid out in the Dayton-Paris Agreement. The Dayton-Paris agreement is very clear about the structure of monetary institutions, but is much more ambiguous about the fiscal structures. In addition, basic government services need to be restored and the infrastructure of government (offices, communications, equipment, and so on) needs to be rehabilitated.

- *Third, managing the transition to a market economy.* The war interrupted the process of economic transformation that had already begun elsewhere in Central and Eastern Europe and in some of the other republics of the former

Yugoslavia. It is important that this process be completed in Bosnia in order to form the basis for sustained growth. As elsewhere in Central and Eastern Europe, much of the increase in output in the medium term will have to come from expansion of service sectors and of light industry, set up by private entrepreneurs. Some of the assets in currently idle State firms may be of use to the private sector; splitting off the useful parts of State enterprises and selling them through simple and rapid privatization mechanisms is needed.

In many cases the three tasks overlap. The new State needs a new body of law, adapted to the requirements of a market economy; but such laws need to take into account the institutional structure laid out in the Dayton-Paris Agreements. Modern tax systems are much more easily built up in a unitary State than in a federal structure with decentralized, or Entity-based institutions, so this will be a special challenge. Privatization, too, will have to be organized at the regional level to avoid debates about unfair asset allocation across communities, despite the potential inefficiencies of multiple privatization agencies.

Yet one cannot dwell on all the difficulties. The agreements reached in Dayton and Paris constitute the only framework to which all parties have consented, and they will have to form the basis of all measures considered. The challenge is to build on these agreements to construct a State and an economic system ready for the market, based on private sector economic activities and with a functioning government that ensures orderly relations between all parties and provides the infrastructure, public goods, and regulatory frameworks that the private sector requires.

Background and Recent Developments

Bosnia and Herzegovina was among the last republics of the former Socialist Federal Republic of Yugoslavia to declare its independence, as the republic's leaders tried to piece together a compromise solution within a confederate structure. With the active encouragement of the major Western countries and of the European Union, which had suggested a referendum, and following the referendum vote in which 67 percent of the population opted for independence, Bosnia and Herzegovina became an independent country in March 1992. International recognition was given to the Republic of Bosnia and Herzegovina by the United Nations and most nations in the months following the referendum. However, the republic's independence was challenged almost immediately by the Yugoslav National Army and local Serb militia, resulting in the four-year war. As a result of the war, about 250,000 people are dead or missing and about three million have had to leave their towns and villages, with about one million seeking refuge abroad. During a brief period in 1993-94, hostilities also broke out between secessionist Croats and the Republic's army. This conflict was largely resolved with the Washington Agreement in early 1994, that established a Federation of Bosnia and Herzegovina between Bosniacs and Croats. On November 21, 1995, a comprehensive peace agreement among all parties was initialed in Dayton, Ohio that establishes a framework for ending the conflict. On December 14, 1995, the peace agreement was formally signed in Paris.

The agreement sets an institutional framework for rebuilding the country. Under the agreement, Bosnia and Herzegovina will be an internationally recognized country consisting of the Bosniac-Croat Federation (Federation of Bosnia and Herzegovina) and the Serb Republic (Republika Srpska). A State government will be responsible for foreign affairs, customs and foreign trade policies, monetary management, and inter-Entity matters on communications, transport, and energy. Other responsibilities, including defense, social services, and social welfare, will be devolved to the Federation and the Serb Republic. Until elections are held in six to nine months, the agreement also confirms the authority of existing government offices and institutions so long as the laws and regulations on which these institutions exercise their competency are consistent with the Constitution agreed to under the agreement.

Infrastructure to implement the peace process was put into place shortly after the signing of the Dayton-Paris peace agreement in Paris. On December 21-22, an international donor conference was convened in Brussels to secure much-needed financial assistance for reconstruction and humanitarian needs during the first quarter of 1996. NATO's implementation forces took over military peacekeeping duties from the United Nations' multilateral force on December 21. On January 4, 1996, the Office of the High Representative began to function in Sarajevo and Brussels. New State and Federation governments were named on January 30 and 31. The withdrawal of the three warring factions behind a zone of separation took place close to schedule, as did the removal of heavy weapons. Most prisoners have been exchanged and the demobilization of soldiers is beginning.

Progress has been somewhat slower on the civilian side. This outcome is to be expected given the complexity of the tasks to be achieved: the organization of free and fair elections, protection of human rights, establishment of a fair and effective police force, building of democratic and pluralistic institutions, return of displaced persons and refugees, and provision of humanitarian and reconstruction assistance. As of late March 1996, the Federation remained largely divided into separate Bosniac majority and Croat majority areas, with separate armies, police, and fiscal administrations. To keep the process of building the Federation on track, a two-day summit was held in Rome in mid-February at which the presidents of Bosnia-Herzegovina, the Republic of Croatia, and the Federal Republic of Yugoslavia reaffirmed their commitment to the Dayton-Paris peace agreement. On March 18, 1996, another agreement between the three parties reaffirmed their intention to implement the peace agreement and committed themselves to specific measures for realizing that objective.

The war has shattered the economy and severely curtailed productive activity. However, this contraction has not occurred uniformly across the country and has not had the same genesis. Output fell most in the Bosniac majority areas due to the destruction of large segments of transport and communications networks, water and energy supplies, and productive assets, as well as loss of human resources. In the Serb majority areas, where the decline was also severe, the economic embargo imposed by the Federal Republic of Yugoslavia and the international community, along with some destruction and damage of basic infrastructure, largely explains the lack of economic activity. Only in the Croat majority areas have production and trade continued, at about 85 percent of the prewar level. Average per capita income in Bosnia and Herzegovina is estimated at about $500, compared with around $1,900 in 1990.

Despite the pain and suffering brought by the war, there has always been hope in the country, even in its darkest moments. Economic life continued throughout the war in places such as Sarajevo and central Bosnia, and there has even been quite successful macroeconomic stabilization since late 1994, as well as encouraging recovery of output since the spring of 1995 in the Federation part of the country, that reflects a turning of energy from political deliberations to growth. With a well-endowed human capital base and an appropriate set of forward-looking policies, Bosnia and Herzegovina could emerge as a successful economy, provided international assistance can be mobilized for the initial reconstruction, and domestic institution-building efforts proceed.

Toward Reconstruction and Recovery

Economic reconstruction and recovery is urgently needed in Bosnia and Herzegovina to give hope and jobs. Experience from countries similarly afflicted by war shows that economic recovery *can* proceed quickly if a number of conditions are satisfied. These conditions generally include: (i) a stable macroeconomic environment conducive to growth and job creation; (ii) a transparent and "market-friendly" legal and regulatory framework, enforced by strong institutions and good coordination within the government, and (iii) sufficient international assistance, official and private, channeled through good organization and coordination mechanisms. Private investment can play a role if basic infrastructure and government services are restored, but requires a relatively stable macroeconomic environment. There are, of course, numerous examples of failure to revive an economy in a postwar environment. The absence of the conditions listed above goes a long way toward explaining the economic collapse in those countries.

Major sources of growth and employment generation in the initial stages of recovery in Bosnia and Herzegovina will have to come from reconstruction-related activities, since domestic market and export capacities are limited. In addition, targeted employment generation programs will be needed. Because significant resources will be provided by donors during the initial stage of economic recovery, a key issue is the design of the aid schemes. It is absolutely critical that reconstruction projects employ Bosnian personnel and companies, and that food aid does not hamper the recovery of agricultural production and the creation of jobs in the rural areas. Equally important in this initial stage of economic recovery is the early adoption by the authorities of a set of measures that can immediately facilitate economic restructuring.

These include measures that promote internal (*intra-* and *inter-Entity*) trade as well as external trade and help reactivate functioning productive assets. Maintaining sound macroeconomic policies in the face of a large inflow of foreign exchange presents a particular problem, and the dynamics of price and real exchange rate movement should be well understood and taken into account in policy formulation. These concerns will require a concerted effort on the part of *both* the government and donors.

Reconstruction:Priorities and Organization

An important focus of the economic recovery program will be job creation and the reconstruction of transport, telecommunications, energy, and other infrastructure damaged by the war, without which it will be impossible to restart production and trade on any significant scale. In parallel, the program must repair water, sewerage, and health facilities without which there will be a continued threat to public health, rehabilitate farms to improve the supply of food and reconstruct housing to relieve acute shortages. Reintegrating demobilized soldiers and the unemployed in the economy is not only an economic necessity but is essential for peace. Financing for these efforts will mostly have to come from abroad. The external financing requirement is currently estimated at $5.1 billion for the initial three or four years.

A coordinated effort by the government and the donor community will be required to deploy these resources, not only for effective targeting and efficiency but also to maximize the positive impact on economic recovery. The government's first step should be to establish an institutional structure that has clearly defined responsibilities for each agency involved in the reconstruction program. The State government has recently set up a Reconstruction Cabinet chaired by the State prime minister and consisting of key ministers at the State level, as well as the Federation prime minister and other key Federation ministers. The Cabinet will define the reconstruction program framework, priorities, and fund-raising strategy. Similarly, the Federation established a Coordination Board and the Serb Republic a Reconstruction Agency to define the needs, funding, and priorities of the reconstruction program at the Entity level. At the sectoral level, line ministries or implementing agencies will be responsible, through the establishment of "project implementation units," for the reconstruction implementation in their areas. This arrangement maintains clear responsibility for key decision-making at the State and Entity levels, yet decentralizes sectoral implementation and help build up institutional capacities. It should provide a good institutional basis for internal coordination of the reconstruction program and for the development of effective implementation capacity.

On the donor side, apart from finding good mechanisms to coordinate amongst themselves to maximize the impact of assistance and minimize the burden of multiple donor programs on the government, there are also important policy issues. Clearly, large-scale economic recovery will not take off if weak demand, resulting from low levels of domestic income and employment in the aftermath of a devastating war, persists. One way to increase aggregate domestic demand is to use donor money in a way that maximizes the employment of domestic companies and local employees for reconstruction projects, large or small. In this respect it is fortunate that Bosnia and Herzegovina has excellent engineering and construction capacity, both for domestic and foreign projects, and that some of its main companies continued operations abroad during the war. Large projects can be designed and undertaken jointly by Bosnia and Herzegovina and foreign companies, while smaller projects should be left for local companies and employees.

Employment Creation and Return of Refugees, Resettlement, and Demobilization

Creating employment is on the critical path to peace and prosperity, in particular to accommodate millions of returning refugees, displaced persons, and demobilized soldiers. In addition to pursuing a policy of employing as many local personnel and local companies as possible in the reconstruction program, creative and diversified programs will be needed to fulfill the tremendous employment requirement facing the country. Programs such as those facilitating *micro and small business creation through credit extension*, technology transfer, information dissemination, and quick privatization of small and functioning assets of State enterprises via simplified mechanisms can be of great importance for alleviating employment pressure as well as stimulating growth.

A variety of *public works programs* in repairing housing for schools and clinics, maintenance of road and street, urban sanitation, water systems, etc. could be of help, and will need donor resources to fund them because of lack of fiscal resources. Training, education and outplacing programs can facilitate reintroduction of these personnel into work life. In designing schemes for demobilization, features such as lump-sum payments for housing repairs, small credit for business activities could be incorporated into the programs to help employment generation.

A donor-financed program of housing construction would also help to stimulate local employment as well as help settle refugees, displaced persons, and demobilized soldiers. Such a program would help generate income and domestic demand by increasing employment to support recovery in production and distribution, and would help contain domestically financed fiscal outlays. Moreover, to the extent that financing housing in Bosnia and Herzegovina offsets the high costs associated with the housing of refugees in many EU countries, spending money on housing construction (and associated water and sewerage sites/facilities) may in fact *save* donors money over the medium term. Private remittances would also be an additional important source of financing for housing repair and employment.

Food Aid

Until now, foreign aid has been channeled mainly in the form of direct government handouts, especially for food aid. As the economic recovery continues, the mechanism for distributing foreign aid should be restructured to minimize its potentially negative effects on the revival of domestic production. In particular, the food aid distribution mechanisms need to be restructured. Donor-supplied food aid, if not organized properly, can discourage domestic food production. Donors should procure a significant share of their food aid from domestic sources of production whenever feasible, such as for cereals, flour, and meat. Doing so would generate a "demand-pull" for the agriculture and agroprocessing sectors in regions such as Herzegovina where farm assets sit idle due to lack of local purchasing power. Moreover, food aid should be *sold* rather than distributed free of charge; those in need of aid could be given targeted income support (see below). Finally, the quantities and types of food aid provided should be monitored carefully and phased out as local agricultural production recovers and commercial food imports develop. This will contribute to the generation of badly needed jobs for the large number of unemployed and displaced persons.

Strengthening Social Assistance Mechanisms

An integral component of the strategy for economic revival is to efficiently deploy scarce resources to help the poor and the socially disadvantaged. By 1995, about 80 percent of the Federation's population had become at least partly dependent on emergency food aid for its survival. A significant portion of the population in the Serb Republic also depends on humanitarian assistance. Despite the anticipated economic recovery, a significant share of the population will continue to remain dependent on social assistance through the medium term. Thus the phasing out of in-kind emergency food aid programs will require the establishment of targeted cash transfer mechanisms to avoid hardship. Temporary programs are required until pension, unemployment, and social assistance systems are restarted.

Facilitating Trade and Reactivating Functioning Assets

Other measures that could be taken by the authorities to help jump-start economic recovery include removing trade barriers that are now in place because of separate intra-Entity and inter-Entity payments and customs administrations, opening up trade routes by implementing the understandings reached in the Washington agreement concerning the port of Ploce, reaching agreements with trading partners for export insurance; and quickly privatizing still-functioning but idle, assets of State enterprises (such as trucks, machines, and sheds). These assets could be split off and sold through simple mechanisms by the enterprises themselves. A major concern at the present is the continued existence of internal checkpoints across Bosnia and Herzegovina and within the Federation that inhibits free and unencumbered movements of goods and donor supplies. Strong and immediate actions are required by all authorities involved to remove these barriers, since donor resources will quickly dry up if they find that their goods are subject to any interventions, and a monitoring and enforcement mechanism, with international support, should be established to ensure that these actions are taken and no new barriers established. The reopening of trade routes, and the reactivation of functioning assets, will be powerful instruments to accelerate job creation both in the industrial and in the services sector.

The Macroeconomics of Economic Recovery

Maintaining macroeconomic stability will be a key requirement for successful recovery and, if experience elsewhere in Eastern Europe is any guide, is a prerequisite for, rather than an enemy of, renewed growth and employment generation. Two key problems are likely to emerge. The first is the threat of a reignition of inflation. The currency board arrangement being put in place for the new central bank sends a good signal that the process of institution building will not interfere with monetary management. However, large expenditure needs and the fragile fiscal situation clearly could threaten the fiscal support needed for the strict monetary policy envisaged under the currency board. Thus establishing a fiscal structure that allows effective control of the government and public sector deficit is a key priority (see below).

The second problem concerns the management of the exchange rate in an environment of strong reconstruction inflows. Experience elsewhere suggests that such activities will put strong upward pressure on the real exchange rate since much of the demand for domestic resources will be directed at the nontraded sector. Prices will likely go up. That in itself is not a problem; as long as the reconstruction effort continues, this is simply a reflection of market realities. However, over time, the exchange rate may become overvalued and uncompetitive. Careful judgment is therefore needed on when inflation is reflecting inappropriate monetary and fiscal policies rather than being a justified real exchange rate adjustment. Several measures can be taken to minimize the degree of real exchange rate appreciation and its adverse consequences. Most important in this regard is the elimination of domestic barriers to the free flow of goods and factor services, including labor, which in turn requires legal and administrative reform in trade, labor markets, and the financial sector.

Building a Viable Structure for Economic Management

The Dayton-Paris Peace Agreement devolves most government responsibilities and the control over revenues from the State to the "constituent Entities"—that is, the Federation of Bosnia and Herzegovina and the Serb Republic. The agreements on decentralized structures for the State and the Federation—the Serb Republic remains unitarily organized—are designed to reduce the scope for the reemergence of major conflict between various groups while preserving a chance for a pluralistic, multicultural society to reemerge. But as the failure of the former Yugoslavia demonstrates, a decentralized structure is only viable if inter-Entity and cantonal links are mutually beneficial. It is essential that the institutional arrangements for macroeconomic control are established, that institutions at the State and the Entity levels are sufficiently strong to fulfill their respective responsibilities in a coordinated and consistent manner, and that there not be too much cross-subsidization between jurisdictions in order to maintain the system's political sustainability. Building a viable structure for economic management within the framework of the peace agreement is therefore essential if Bosnia and Herzegovina is to continue on the road of reconstruction and prosperity.

Building this new structure will involve two tasks. First, the government must rapidly build a core set of State and Entity institutions with competent staff in order to establish credibility for the new structures and foster cooperative behavior. Particularly important institutional arrangements that need to be established or consolidated in a fairly short period include, at the State level, a central bank to provide a common means of payments, customs administration arrangements to ensure uniform tariff rates and customs procedures, payments linkages to facilitate direct settlement of transactions. On the Federation side, this includes Federation customs and tax administrations, a Federation payments bureau, and a Federation bank licensing and supervision agency. On the Serb Republic side, this will require transforming or establishing new institutions for a market economy, including an independent bank supervision agency. Second, the authorities must clarify fiscal arrangements between the State and its constituent Entities and between the Federation and its cantons for revenue and expenditure responsibilities across levels of government, as well as establish intergovernmental revenue redistribution mechanisms.

Building Government Institutions

For Bosnia and Herzegovina to be successful as a pluralistic society, it is crucial that viable institutional arrangements for economic control be established at the State and Entity levels. The peace agreement assigned to the State all the responsibilities needed for Bosnia and Herzegovina to be internationally recognized as one State. It also called for the acceleration of building the Federation as one of the two functioning Entities within Bosnia and Herzegovina. In late 1995 specific steps were agreed to strengthen the Federation. The separation of governments between the State and the Federation occurred in late January 1996 with the establishment of separate cabinet ministries and ministers for all the State-level and Federation-level ministries, but all the cantons and key economic institutions of the Federation have yet to be established. Commitment to these institution-building measures was reconfirmed by the parties to the Dayton-Paris agreement at the Rome meeting on February 18, 1996 and at the Ge*neva meeting on March 18, 1996*.

Key Institutional Arrangements at the State Level. Establishing a State-level central bank is critical to the new State. The Constitution provides considerable guidance on how the central bank will function. It indicates that it will be the *only* authority for monetary policy and for issuing currency in Bosnia and Herzegovina, that it will function as a currency board during its first six years, and that during those six years the bank's governor will be recommended to the presidency by the management of the International Monetary Fund, and will not be a citizen of Bosnia and Herzegovina or any neighboring State. The new central bank will play an important role in improving economic conditions in Bosnia and Herzegovina: it will promote confidence in the ability of various governments to maintain economic stability, improve capacity for external debt management, and, most importantly, facilitate trade and financial flows throughout the country. *Banking supervision* should also be coordinated—or ideally, unified—to provide a uniform set of rules and regulations for all banks operating within Bosnia and Herzegovina. Similarly, *payments systems* between the two Entities should be linked. Initially they could be linked in the way the separate payments systems of the two areas of the Federation were linked in November 1995. Finally, *customs and trade policies* should be coordinated to promote a common open trade regime without quantitative restrictions and to reduce divergence of tariff rates. In this context the discrepancies that exist between the trade regime of the Federation and that of the Serb Republic will have to be addressed. Common customs procedures will have to be adopted once the Serb Republic establishes its customs checkpoints on the country's eastern borders with the Federal Republic of Yugoslavia.

Key Institutions for the Federation. Major tasks for institution-building are required in the Federation to make it possible to have a unified system for effective economic management. Key institutions that need to be established immediately or in very near future include unified customs and tax administrations, unified payment system, and a unified banking supervision agency. *Unified Federation customs and tax administrations* will eliminate intra-Federation trade barriers and create a viable and visibly unified Federation government and fiscal system. The most important steps in this regard include establishment of headquarters and naming of directors for the Federation Tax Administration and Federation Customs Administration, elimination of internal borders within the Federation, channeling of tax and customs revenues to Federation government accounts, appointment of international observer and audit teams as an interim measure to ensure that the new procedures of the unified Federation Customs Administration are being properly observed, and merging of financial police with the customs and tax administration.

Full unification of the payments systems is necessary to complement the unification of the tax and customs administrations, and to help establish a unified financial system in the Federation. Key steps in the next few months include appointment of the director, deputy director, and senior staff of a unified Federal Payments Bureau, development of plans for the harmonization of procedures in all branches and modernization of equipment, and beginning implementation of such plans before the end of the year.

A Federation Banking Agency is needed to provide the basis for uniform bank licensing and regulatory standards throughout the Federation and to permit participation on an equal basis in domestic and international transactions of banks in both parts of the Federation. Draft legislation to reform banking sector regulations and establish a Federation Banking Agency has been prepared and needs to be finalized by the authorities and submitted to Parliament.

Establishment of cantonal governments is a key element of the peace agreement that first requires that agreement be reached on the boundaries of each of the cantons to be established. Appropriate legislation reflecting that agreement needs to be drafted and approved by the Federation Parliament.

Key Institutions for the Serb Republic. Since the Serb Republic has maintained a unitary structure and has already had central institutions, the key task is to adapt these institutions toward serving a market-oriented economy, which Serb authorities have explicitly stated as their key reform objective. However, one institution that needs to be established separately is a Banking Supervision Agency that will be required once the central banking function is taken over at the State level.

Financing the Start-up of Government Institutions. Establishing the key new government institutions, particularly for the State and Federation governments, involves significant up-front costs, including the cost of equalizing and raising salaries in the key institutions to sufficient levels. One possibility is to fund base salaries at the State and Entity levels based on uniform (State-wide or Entity-wide) scales. The base salaries could be supplemented at each level using local resources (for example, topping up of base salaries by the cantons for civil servants at the Federation and the State levels). In addition, the need for adequately equipping these institutions implies significant first-year operating costs. Donor-provided funding should be identified to help cover financing for these outlays.

Toward Viable Fiscal Arrangements

The peace agreement is clear about the structure of monetary institutions but is much more ambiguous about fiscal structures, particularly concerning fiscal arrangements within the Federation. This imprecision raises important questions about the assignment of expenditure and revenue responsibilities across different levels of government and the question of intergovernmental fiscal redistribution. These questions must be satisfactorily dealt with in designing the new fiscal structure, so that it functions efficiently without reigniting economic and political conflicts.

Fiscal Arrangements at the State Level. The division of fiscal responsibility between the State and its two constituent Entities was outlined in the Dayton-Paris agreements. However, many details and mechanisms have yet to be concretized. Under the framework an *asymmetrical* fiscal arrangement for the State will emerge. On the Federation side there will be a fairly decentralized tax and fiscal system with significant taxing and spending powers devolved to the cantons, with the Federation government responsible mainly for those areas that have Federation-wide impact, such as defense and trade. On the Serb Republic side a more centralized fiscal system, similar to the current structure, will likely continue.

Since taxing power will reside with the two constituent Entities of the State, the consistency and coordination on tax policy and administration is a major issue. Some taxes, such as the value-added tax, cannot be imposed at a subnational level unless internal borders are imposed, which is clearly not advisable. Likewise, customs administrations and policies have to be consistent and coordinated in order to provide uniformity in protection and undistorted customs revenue collection. Otherwise internal borders would have to be established as well.

Under the peace agreement, the State government's responsibilities will be important but limited, since defense and social transfers are not included in the State's list of Constitutional responsibilities. The State government's budget will be small, financing mostly the operating cost of the State administration. It is to be financed entirely by contributions from its two Entities, the Bosniac-Croat Federation (two-thirds) and the Serb Republic (one-third), drawing initially from the customs revenues in each Entity. Such a system has the inherent risk of leaving the State vulnerable to the willingness of transferring revenue by the Entities. The peace agreement provides that in the future, subject to the approval of the State Parliament, the State will be able to impose its own taxes.

Since the State is the internationally recognized Entity and international relations are the domain of the State government, foreign borrowing and foreign debt service should be coordinated by the State government, and channeled from the State budget to final beneficiaries, including the Entity governments which could be borrowing directly from abroad as well. However, under the initial design of the peace agreement, financing for debt service will have to come from additional contributions from the constituent Entities.

Fiscal Arrangements of the Federation. Assignment of functions and revenues for the Federation should aim at having a small but strong Federation government and canton administrations with enough fiscal discretion and fiscal power to accommodate the heterogeneity of the Federation. Here, it is important to differentiate between the level of government that imposes the tax and undertakes its collection and administration, and the level of government that actually receives the tax revenue. Different options exist for organizing the revenue system, tax administration and allocating tax revenues. It is advisable that tax administration of the key taxes needing a uniform design be centralized at the federal level; purely local and cantonal taxes can be collected at those levels, respectively. It is also advisable that expenditure assignments be determined before proceeding too far in concretely assigning taxes to lower levels, since it may be hard to change tax assignments at a later stage.

Efficient Allocation of Responsibilities. Four criteria are recommended to determine the optimal assignment of public functions to different levels of government: the potential for economies of scale, the existence of interregional spillovers, variations in preferences, and the desire for equalization and tolerance for cross-subsidies. There are tradeoffs among these criteria. The Federation Constitution has already assigned several functions to the Federation including defense, federal police, justice, and customs administration. Additional functions that could be assigned to the Federation are discussed in chapter III.

Efficient Assignment of Revenues. As a rule, each level of government should have sufficient revenue capacity to fund the services for which it is responsible. In considering the assignment of taxes among different levels of government, it is also important to differentiate among the separate steps of the taxation process. These include collecting, auditing, and enforcement, referred to collectively as tax administration; definition of tax bases; setting of tax rates; and tax "ownership". The level of government in charge of collecting a tax need not be the same level that defines the tax base, sets the tax rate, or owns the tax revenues. In fact, it is recommended that for the most important taxes, definition of the tax base, setting of basic tax rates, and undertaking of tax collection all be done at the Federation level. In addition, customs tax and excises should be exclusively owned by the Federation government, while the personal income tax, corporate income tax, and value-added tax could be shared between the Federation government and cantons.

User Charges. Users of services should pay for services provided to the extent possible. This principle argues for user fees wherever they are technically feasible without violating other principles of equity and equal access. The expansion and establishment of additional user fees is strongly recommended. This policy not only reduces government expenditure, therefore reducing taxing requirements, it also allows for more active citizen participation in the management of public services. Well-designed social pricing mechanisms that address the needs of the poor (such as lifeline pricing, in-kind transfers, or cash transfers) should be an integral part of this cost recovery policy.

Intergovernmental Grants and Revenue Redistribution. Whatever design is eventually adopted, some imbalance between revenue and expenditure within fiscal units is inevitable. Thus it may be necessary to develop an intergovernmental grants or a revenue-sharing system. However, the current level of tolerance for interregional subsidies is low, if not nil. Given the history of the former Yugoslavia, great care must be taken in designing an intergovernmental transfer system to minimize potential sources of political tension. Nonetheless, grant schemes are likely to be needed. These could be based on the redistribution of the proceeds from either a single tax or a pool of tax revenues. The most important thing is that the formula applied to distribute funds across municipalities or cantons be based on objective and transparent indicators. A system of grants based on negotiated formulas or ad hoc procedures would be particularly inappropriate for Bosnia and Herzegovina.

Commission on Fiscal Intergovernmental Relations. Three significant problems can be expected from the establishment of a federation fiscal system. First, fiscal imbalances will arise whatever system is chosen, and these need to be addressed. Second, there must be adequate information on which to base decisions about proper tax base sharing, tax assignment, and intergovernmental transfers. Third, there are significant variations in budgeting procedures within the Federation. The establishment of a Commission on Fiscal Intergovernmental Relations is strongly recommended to address these problems.

Fiscal Arrangements and Policies of the Serb Republic In one respect, issues in reforming the Serb Republic's fiscal structure are different from those of the Federation because it is expected that the unitary structure of the current system will continue. In other respect, however, it will face similar challenges as the Federation. These concern a) establishment of a system of user charges for public goods and services; b) establishment of effective customs administration and coordination with the Federation on policies and procedures; c) rationalization of the fiscal relation between the Republican government and municipalities; d) pension and health finance reforms (see section IV). More review will be needed before concrete proposals can be made concerning reform of fiscal structure in the Serb Republic.

Toward Setting up a Market Economy

Basic Strategy for Recovery and Role of the Government

It is tempting to argue that special conditions in Bosnia and Herzegovina would favor a direct government involvement in increasing production through the restarting of the State-owned enterprises. Nevertheless, growth and job creation in Bosnia, apart from that driven by the reconstruction program, will most likely come from expansion in the services sector and light industry, set up by private entrepreneurs. Therefore, the basic strategy for economic revival should be a reliance on the private sector as the main engine of increased production and employment. The government's extreme fiscal predicament also leaves no alternative to private sector activity if the current macroeconomic stability is to be sustained—the resources are simply not there for any large scale government investment or intervention. In these circumstances, donors will need to address employment generation as an integral part of the reconstruction program.

The State's role under a private sector-led economic development strategy is not unimportant, but refocused. In fact, how the government functions and what policies it implements is critical to fostering a private sector-based economic recovery. It should concentrate on maintaining a sound macroeconomic environment; on establishing a sound legal, regulatory, and institutional framework that promotes smooth functioning of free markets; and on providing essential public goods and social services, such as defense, public order, and basic education and health care. Furthermore, the government must undertake reforms that facilitate the systemic transformation of the economy and enhance efficient resource allocation, particularly in the area of public finance reform (including pension, health, and education finance) and privatization of banks and enterprises.

Bank and Enterprise Reforms

Sustained recovery will not be possible without effective resource mobilization and deployment. This, in turn, requires financial sector reform. Large amounts of inherited bad loans and foreign exchange deposit liabilities have to be removed to free banks from the burden of the past and to allow them to make loans based on the financial viability of current ventures. At the same time large and inefficient State enterprises have to be closed or restructured and privatized. The legacy of social ownership and self-management, although temporarily replaced by direct government control during the war, continues to generate inappropriate incentives on decision making for production and investments. In addition, the prewar linkage between enterprises and banks—enterprises owned the major banks, which made loans to the enterprise owners—if unreformed, will continue to cause major misallocation of resources when investment resumes. Thus bank and enterprise reform efforts should focus on privatizing, through a variety of methods, banks and enterprises. At the same time, legal and regulatory frameworks need to be put in place to ensure effective market competition and to prevent, in the banking sector, major bank failures. The government's key role during the transition period is to manage this process of privatization, to implement legal and regulatory frameworks for private sector development, and to promote competition.

The Medium-Term Legal Framework. Setting up a comprehensive legal framework at the State and the Entity level for market activities is of primary importance for the medium-term development of a market economy. Wherever possible, a *framework* for these laws and regulations should be set up at the State level to provide uniformity. If legislation is set up at the Entity level, consistency and harmonization of this legislation across Entities will be required.

Further legislation is needed to complement and enhance the effectiveness of the laws already adopted. *Property laws* should set clear rules of ownership and control. *Contract laws* and related procedures for dispute resolution are needed to establish a framework for commercial bargaining and to ensure the fair enforcement of private contracts. *Company* and *foreign investment laws* should provide for relatively easy entry of new enterprises into the market, while *bankruptcy law* needs to establish a mechanism for exit. *Regulatory policies* should address market failures, whether inhibiting the distortions of unregulated monopolies, forcing firms to disclose information needed by the market, or providing incentives to internalize environmental costs. The *labor law* should set basic ground rules for employment and industrial relations, including the facilitation of labor shedding by enterprises, supported by national social support and assistance policies if needed. Restrictions and barriers to labor mobility, such as complicated labor shedding procedures, expensive severance payments, and requirements relating to long notification periods and to finding alternative employment, should be removed with a view to facilitating the restructuring of banks and enterprises. Finally, *accounting and auditing laws* and standards based on international rules need to be introduced to provide the basis for compilation and disclosure of uniform and meaningful financial information.

In the financial sector, in addition to the introduction of the new central bank law and new commercial banking laws, other banking regulations are also necessary. These include regulations on licensing standards such as capital entry requirement, scope of operations, shareholder and management requirements, and reporting requirements, as well as regulations on loan classification, interest treatment, restriction of loan concentration to large borrowers and internal borrowers, limits on foreign exchange operations and exposure, and credit policy and procedures. The introduction of a deposit insurance scheme, properly financed and supervised, would contribute greatly to restoring confidence in the banking system. In the medium term laws on nonbank financial institutions and capital market development would be required, to provide alternate financing for the growing private sector. Some of these regulations have already been adopted by each Entity.

Immediate measures on bank and enterprise reforms. Immediate bank and enterprise reforms should focus on removing the negative impact of inherited bad loans and large frozen foreign exchange deposit liabilities, and on promoting investment and production. Three principles should guide bank and enterprise reforms. First, stock liabilities and non-performing assets should be separated from current operations so that they do not impede reactivating economic activities. Second, the fiscal costs of settling the outstanding liabilities embedded in the banking sector should be minimized. Third, a decentralized approach to privatization should be pursued. The design and implementation of the program can vary so long as these principles are broadly observed.

Settling claims. A particular problem is the large number of claims on the government, including claims of individuals (unpaid wages and pensions, restitution for postwar nationalization, claims on frozen foreign currency accounts, claims for damage and other losses arising from the war) and claims between and among the government and socially-owned institutions (bad bank loans, enterprise-government arrears, and interenterprise arrears). Settling all these claims from available fiscal resources is well beyond the government's fiscal capacity. Therefore no major fiscal resources should be provided for the settlement of claims. A substantial portion of the claims of individuals could be settled by exchanging them for privatization certificates that can be used along with cash for privatization transactions.

Settlement through the provision of privatization certificates could be envisaged for three types of claims: (i) claims equal to the value of bank deposits in foreign exchange that were frozen in 1991; (ii) restitution claims, where these cannot or should not be settled in kind with the property being claimed; and (iii) claims by government employees and pensioners for their wage and pension arrears, and claims by veterans based on their length of service and the degree of injury or other personal loss they may have suffered. These privatization certificates could later be used, together with cash, to purchase publicly-owned assets that could be offered for sale in the near future, including housing, agricultural and forest land, enterprises and commercial banks.

A regional approach to privatization. Given the institutional structure of the State and the initial steps already taken, a regionally based, flexible approach toward enterprise and bank restructuring and privatization may be most appropriate. Under this approach privatization programs will be implemented regionally (at the Serb Republic level and at group of cantons, canton, or local levels within the Federation) through regional privatization agencies, while all claims, including bad bank claims on enterprises, interenterprise arrears, frozen foreign exchange deposit claims, and the claims on government for wage and pension arrears, restitution, or war-related claims are transferred from the current institutions to a settlement mechanism to be established. This approach would drastically reduce enterprise debts and remove bank liabilities (up to a point) from the balance sheet, substantially cleaning enterprises and banks. In this framework, a clear preference should be given to rapid privatization schemes.

Bank and financial sector reform issues. Reviving the banking system will be key to a speedy restoration of economic activity in Bosnia and Herzegovina. The banking system has been reduced to an agent for the execution of payments within a very unsatisfactory mechanism. The banking system's intermediary role and its corporate governance role have basically come to a standstill. Banks not only suffer from portfolio deterioration due to enterprise loan servicing difficulties, but they also carry a considerable burden as a consequence of the disorderly breakup of the former Yugoslavia. Frozen foreign exchange deposits and claims on the former central bank of Yugoslavia have to be separated from their existing balance sheet and the latter dealt with within negotiations between sovereign nations. As for bad loans, Bosnia's extreme circumstance may make collection a hopeless endeavor. Therefore, they too should be removed from banks' balance sheets.

There is one positive element to restructuring: unlike the rest of Central and Eastern Europe, the former Yugoslavia long had a functioning decentralized commercial banking system, so there is no need to construct it from scratch. However, the pre-1990 banks suffered from severely deficient corporate governance structures, with major borrowers often acting as owners too. Such structures must be avoided at all costs if banks are to impose hard budget constraints on troubled borrowers. Furthermore, legal frameworks, regulatory structures, and information systems are all essential and need to be either created or, where they exist, adapted to the new environment.

Banking regulation and supervision It is crucial that legal and supervisory frameworks consistent with modern banking regulations be established and supervisory capacity developed early on. Reform experience in other Central and Eastern European countries has demonstrated that if financially restructured banks stay under direct government ownership for too long, or if effective regulatory and supervisory frameworks are not put into practice, it is highly likely that bank losses will recur and the government will have to intervene again. An active drive to privatize or liquidate the restructured banks as well as regulatory and supervisory strengthening should therefore be the key priorities for banking reform.

Medium-Term Prospects and Financing Requirements

Considerable external financing is needed to normalize Bosnia and Herzegovina's relations with external creditors, as well as to cover the reconstruction requirements. This normalization involves both the clearance of outstanding arrears as well as the restructuring of the remaining debt. A strategy to resolve the debt problem should seek immediate relief on debt service obligations, as well as a permanent reduction of total indebtedness, thereby allowing the economy to function on its own over the short and medium term. Cash flow relief from external donors is particularly important to ensure a significant positive transfer into the country during the recovery and to reduce the debt service burden to a reasonable level. However, without a comprehensive debt workout, including a substantial net present value reduction on consolidated debt service with Paris Club creditors and substantial debt stock reduction with London Club creditors, it is not likely that Bosnia and Herzegovina will return to a creditworthy status for some time, reducing any chance that private capital will be forthcoming to replace aid and become a significant source of capital inflow for economic growth and employment generation.

Given the uncertainty of the situation, any macroeconomic scenario must be seen as tentative, and essentially an illustration of the possible evolution of the economy under certain assumptions including the political environment, external financing, economic policies, institution building and the implementation of the reconstruction program. Recovery in the agriculture and service sectors, and starting up of housing and infrastructure reconstruction, coupled with significant inflow of donor assistance are expected to improve Bosnia and Herzegovina's GDP substantially in 1996, provided that good policies are followed and institution-building efforts proceed well. Further improvement in economic performance will depend a strong economic reform program, effective strengthening of institutional capacity for economic management, continued strong international financial and governmental assistance, including favorable Paris and London debt deals, and, of course, continued progress of the peace process. Only if these conditions are maintained on a sustained basis is it possible to project continued vigorous economic recovery of, say, 10 percent a year for the rest of the decade. But even under this optimistic scenario, GDP per capita and exports would recover to only about two-thirds of their prewar level by the year 2000.

Conclusion

An extraordinary effort will be required of the people of Bosnia and Herzegovina and its government in the postwar rebuilding of their country. Viable institutional arrangements for economic management need to be swiftly established. The economy has to be revived speedily to create jobs and to accommodate rising expectations while macroeconomic stability is maintained. A great deal of financial assistance by the international community will be required to support reconstruction, implement stabilization and structural reform measures, and normalize international financial relations. Donors are urged to join together to make every effort to support Bosnia and Herzegovina in the process of reconstruction, and to work with the Bosnians to develop speedy and creative programs to support this immense undertaking. There will be risks in the process. Even with strong external support, the process of reintegration will not be easy, and the international community must be aware of the difficulties that lie ahead. But without a concerted effort, there can be no hope for recovery and a durable peace, and Bosnia will remain troubled and potentially unstable, and blight the prospects for a future of peace and economic progress for all countries in the Balkan region.

I.   BACKGROUND AND RECENT DEVELOPMENTS

The disintegration of the Socialist Federal Republic of Yugoslavia near the end of 1991 led to dramatic political and economic developments that radically altered all aspects of life in Bosnia and Herzegovina. These developments can be divided into three phases. The first phase began with the outbreak of war in May 1992 and ended with the Washington Agreement in March 1994, marking the cessation of hostilities between Bosniac and Croat forces, the establishment of the Bosniac-Croat Federation, and the consolidation of the Serb Republic. The second phase covered the period until the conclusion of the Dayton-Paris Peace Talks in November 1995. Although hostilities were still ongoing during this phase, it was also marked by initial efforts to build the Federation and the beginnings of economic recovery. The third phase covers the period since the signing of the Dayton-Paris Peace Agreement in December 1995. The Peace Agreement establishes a framework for rebuilding a multicultural, pluralistic society in Bosnia and Herzegovina, involving various military, political, and institutional aspects.

Descent into War and Economic Collapse

Following a decade of mounting internal tensions that started in early 1980s, the disintegration of the former Yugoslavia accelerated with the secession of Slovenia and Croatia. Both countries declared their independence in 1991 and were subsequently recognized by the international community as independent states. Discussions on the sovereignty of Bosnia and Herzegovina between its three regionally-based political parties—the Party for Democratic Action, the Croat Democratic Community, and the Serb Democratic Party— began shortly after the first free elections in Yugoslavia in November 1990. Bosniac and Croat politicians supported the principle of Bosnian sovereignty; Serb leaders opposed it. In November 1991, the European Union's Badinter Commission indicated that the Republic of Bosnia and Herzegovina satisfied the necessary conditions for being recognized as an independent republic by the European Union, provided that the desire for independence was confirmed by popular referendum.   This referendum was held on March 1, 1992.   The two-thirds of the adult population that voted almost unanimously favored independence. The other, nonvoting third of the population, however, largely comprised the Bosnian Serbs, many of whom had decided to boycott the referendum.

Bosnia and Herzegovina was recognized as an independent State by the member countries of the European Union and the United States and became a United Nations member under Security Council Resolution 755 on May 22, 1992 (box 1.1).   The country's independence and territorial integrity were immediately challenged by local Serb militias and the Yugoslav National Army, however. By the end of 1992, almost two-thirds of Bosnia and Herzegovina's territory was occupied by rebel Serb forces. In the spring of 1993 fighting broke out between the allied Bosnian Croat and Bosniac groups. A partial political settlement was reached on February 25, 1994, when a cease-fire was declared by the Bosniac and Bosnian Croat forces, followed by the Washington agreements of March 1994.

Box 1.1 Territory and population

Bosnia and Herzegovina lies on the Balkan Peninsula, bounded on the north, west, and south by the Republic of Croatia and on the east by the Federal Republic of Yugoslavia. It comprises a territory of 51,129 square kilometers, making it about one and a half times the size of Belgium. The prewar population was 4,366,000 people. Bosniacs, who comprised 43.7 percent of the population in 1991, are majority Muslims. Serbs (31.4 percent of the population) largely belong to the Serbian Orthodox Church. Croats (17.3 percent of the population) belong to the Roman Catholic Church. The remaining 7.6 percent of the population declared themselves Yugoslavs or other nationalities in the 1991 Census.

Mountains traverse much of the country. Extensions of the Dinaric Alps form its western border with Croatia and cross its northern part. The southwestern part lies within the Kars, a barren limestone plateau broken by depressions and ridges. While much of the northern and central portions of the country are heavily forested, the south has flat regions of fertile soil that are used as farmland. The country has about 20 kilometers of coastline along the Adriatic Sea but no major port. Its maritime trade has been mainly channeled through the port of Ploce in Croatia. Natural resources include timber, coal, salt, manganese, silver, lead, iron ore, and copper.

Sarajevo, the historic capital of Bosnia and Herzegovina, has for centuries been a vibrant cultural and economic center where Muslim, Catholic, Orthodox, and Jewish communities have coexisted in peace, intermarried, and shared a sense of pride in their city, generally recognized as one of the most beautiful in southwestern Europe. Today, the city is reunited but has suffered considerable damage and lost much of its original diversity.

The Federation Is Formed and the Serb Republic Is Consolidated

The Washington Agreements of March 1994 led to the formation of the Federation of Bosnia and Herzegovina, whose Constitution organizes the territories with a majority of Bosniac and Bosnian Croat populations into cantons as federal units. The territories with a predominantly Serb population established a separate Entity, the Serb Republic, with government headquarters in Pale and Banja Luka. Among other things, the Federation Constitution outlines the division of responsibilities between the Federation government and the cantons and municipalities, as well as the assignment of some taxes. Except for the responsibilities that were subsequently elevated to the State government, this division of responsibilities was largely confirmed by the State Constitution agreed under the Dayton-Paris Peace Agreement.

The implementation of the new Federation arrangements, however, has been slow. Trade relations between both parts of the Federation have resumed, some major utilities were rehabilitated with external assistance, and the European Union (EU) initiated its administration of Mostar. But many important decisions on tax and spending assignments within the Federation have not been made. Also, the unification of various Federation institutions called for under the Constitution (such as customs and tax administrations and the process of forming the new cantons) have been slow at best. By March 1996, only two cantonal units had a cantonal assembly, a governor, and a draft budget; no significant progress was made in establishing a truly unified Federation Customs Administration; and payments systems were linked only through primitive arrangements. In part, the implementation of these agreements was hampered by continued displacements of the population on account of ongoing hostilities with the Bosnian Serbs. Continuing distrust between Bosnian Croats and Bosniacs, especially in Mostar, has also played a role.

Still, the economic situation in the Federation began to improve noticeably after mid-1994, reflecting both more stable macroeconomic conditions and the cessation of hostilities between the members of the Federation. The hyperinflation experienced in the Bosniac majority area was halted with the adoption of a successful stabilization program in July 1994. The retail price index fell by 40 percent during 1995, with a sharp decline in traded goods prices but a large increase in the price index of domestic services. Production indicators in most economic subsectors increased by 200-600 percent in 1995 relative to 1994.

Box 1.2 The prewar economy

The former Yugoslavia's economy grew by an average of 5.5 percent a year from 1960-90. Though this rising prosperity was broadly shared in the 1980s, Bosnia and Herzegovina remained one of the poorer republics in the former Yugoslavia. Its GDP reached $8.3 billion, or around $1,900 per capita, in 1990 — considerably below the $6,500 of Slovenia but more than Macedonia's $1,400. The economy was more open and market-oriented than other socialist economies; it had a highly educated labor force, and more than half its export products were sold to Western markets for hard currency.

The economy was fairly diversified, with a large industrial base and a highly capable entrepreneurial class that produced complex goods such as aircraft and machine tools. More than half of output and employment was generated by the industrial sector, which concentrated in the energy and raw material producing sectors (especially electricity generation, wood production, coal and bauxite mining, and coke production), as well as textiles, leather, footwear, and machinery and electrical equipment. In the service sector, Bosnia and Herzegovina developed a strong capacity in civil engineering. Almost 500 engineering and construction companies operated out of Bosnia and Herzegovina before the war, generating roughly 7 percent of GDP.

The economic situation also started to improve in the Serb Republic after March 1994, once the Federal Republic of Yugoslavia adopted a stabilization program involving a fixed exchange rate policy and strict supporting policies (known as the Avramovic plan). In August 1994, however, the Serb Republic's economy suffered a major setback when Yugoslavia joined other nations in imposing sanctions mandated by the United Nations. These sanctions included an embargo on external trade, a cutoff of telecommunications, the freezing of financial accounts and assets of the Serb Republic in Yugoslavia, and tight restrictions on border crossings. The Serb Republic responded by tightening control of expenditures, raising tax rates and improving collections, and directing credit and supplies to maintain a minimum of domestic production. Because direct domestic and external borrowing were not available, fiscal accounts were balanced on a cash basis, though there was substantial accumulation of arrears.

The Dayton-Paris Peace Agreement

Armed hostilities between the Federation and the Serb Republic came to an end with a cease-fire agreement in October 1995 that led to the peace agreement initialed in Dayton on November 21, 1995, and signed in Paris on December 14, 1995. The agreement establishes an institutional framework for rebuilding the country. Under the agreement, Bosnia and Herzegovina is an internationally recognized State comprising two Entities: the Federation of Bosnia and Herzegovina and the Serb Republic. The Federation is divided into cantons. The Federation, comprising the Bosniac majority and Croat majority areas as well as some mixed cantons, accounts for 51 percent of the territory of Bosnia and Herzegovina. The Serb Republic, comprising the Serb majority area and the other 49 percent of the state's territory (with a population of about one million persons), remains organized in a unitary, centralized fashion, with the Entity-level government dealing directly with the municipalities (box 1.3).

Under the Dayton-Paris Constitution, the State government of Bosnia and Herzegovina will be responsible mainly for foreign policy, foreign trade, customs and immigration policy, monetary policy, and matters of inter-Entity concern, such as air traffic control. All other responsibilities belong to the governments of each Entity or to the cantonal and municipal governments beneath them. The complete establishment and operation of the Federation government, as well as of the canton governments, are essential elements of the Dayton-Paris Agreement.

The main State-level governmental institutions of Bosnia and Herzegovina are:

- A bicameral **legislature** consisting of a fifteen-person House of Peoples selected from the two Entity legislatures and a forty-two-person House of Representatives directly elected from each Entity. Two-thirds of each House will come from the Federation and one-third from the Serb Republic.

- An **executive** branch whose highest powers reside in a three-person presidency (one to be directly elected by the Serb Republic and two by the Federation) and a Council of Ministers, which cover responsibilities described above.

- A **judiciary** branch whose highest powers reside in a constitutional court that decides constitutional disputes (including those on appeal from Entity courts).

- A central bank, organized as a currency board and led by a governing board consisting of one governor and three other members (to be appointed by the presidency at the recommendation of the International Monetary Fund), that determines monetary policy. All elected and appointed offices entail procedures that aim to ensure balanced Bosniac, Croat, and Serb representation. Until elections are held in September 1996, the Peace Agreement confirms the authority of existing governments, whose offices and institutions will continue to function as long as their laws and procedures do not conflict with the State Constitution.

Box 1.3 The constitutional division of government responsibilities

Under the Constitution, major government responsibilities are divided among the four levels of government.

The *State government* has exclusive responsibility for foreign policy, foreign trade policy, customs policy, monetary policy, immigration and asylum policies, air traffic control, payment of international financial obligations incurred with the consent of both Entities, and inter-Entity transport, communications, and law enforcement. The State government has no independent revenue sources and will finance its activities entirely from transfers from the two Entities—two-thirds from the Federation and one-third from the Serb Republic — that should cover the budget approved by the State Parliament. The State may also eventually control any new revenue sources that are specified by Parliament in the future.

The *Entity governments* will each have exclusive responsibility in their territories over defense (there are currently three armies: one in the Serb Republic, and two in the Federation, one Bosnian-Croat and one Bosniac, but supposed to have one head for defense in the Federation), internal affairs (including police), environmental policies, economic and social sector policies (such as agriculture, industry, and health), refugees and displaced persons, reconstruction programs and justice, tax, and customs administration. To carry out these responsibilities, each Entity will be given ownership of the customs duties and excise taxes collected in its territory.

The *canton governments* — in the case of the Federation — are responsible for all other matters not granted explicitly to the Entity governments. These include education, culture, housing, public services, local land use, and social transfer expenditures. Each canton is authorized by the federal constitution to delegate its responsibilities to the municipalities in its territory. To finance these activities, the cantons are given ownership of sales, income, and property taxes, as well as of the fees charged for public services.

The municipal governments are granted "self-rule on local matters", including all responsibilities delegated to them by the canton. In the case of municipalities with a majority population that is different from that of the canton as a whole, the canton must delegate all responsibilities described in the preceding paragraph to the municipal government.

Much has happened in Bosnia and Herzegovina since the signing of the Dayton-Paris Peace Agreement in Paris on December 14, 1995. Compliance with the military aspects of the Agreement has been good. Despite initial difficulties and inclement winter conditions, NATO's Implementation Forces troops were deployed on the ground. The withdrawal of the three parties' forces behind a zone of separation took place close to schedule, as did the removal of heavy weapons. Most of prisoners have been exchanged and the demobilization of soldiers is under way.

Progress has been slower on the civilian side. This is to be expected given the complexity of the tasks to be achieved: the organization of free and fair elections, protection of human rights, establishment of a fair and effective police force, building of democratic and multiethnic institutions, return of displaced persons and refugees, and provision of humanitarian and reconstruction assistance.

The preparation for free and fair elections is under way under the supervision of the Organization for Security and Cooperation in Europe. The United Nations High Commissioner for Refugees has drafted a detailed operational plan for the return of displaced persons and refugees. The first steps in the establishment of democratic institutions were taken on January 30, when a new government was formed for the State of Bosnia and Herzegovina. A few days later new governments for the Federation and the Serb Republic were announced. Humanitarian assistance continues, and the reconstruction and economic recovery program is under way. To coordinate and facilitate these civilian aspects of the peace accords as mandated under the peace agreement, the Office of the High Representative has been set up. Under this office a Joint Civilian Commission - comprising representatives from the State government and the governments of the Federation and Serb Republic, the Implementation Forces' commander, and key agencies working in Bosnia and Herzegovina — has met regularly to ensure progress on implementation.

More important, the daily lives of the Bosnian people have been substantially improved by the implementation of the Peace Agreement. Children who were kept indoors during Sarajevo's long years of siege can now begin to have hope of a normal childhood. People who have seen nothing but food aid packaged up to thirty years ago now enjoy real meals. Sarajevo is no longer under siege. Water, electricity, and heat have been restored in many communities. Roads are opening and markets are functioning. Supplies of essential goods are flowing more freely, resulting in prices falling from the astronomical levels they reached during the war. Freedom of movement is improving and the daily fear of snipers has subsided.

The Dayton-Paris Peace Agreement ended Europe's most destructive war in the past fifty years (box 1.4). The agreement is the first step toward reintegration and reconstruction for Bosnia and Herzegovina, a task whose outcome could cement or shatter the fragile peace. The positive conclusion of the Peace Talks and the cessation of hostilities have placed the need for economic recovery onto center stage. In this regard Bosnia and Herzegovina faces three major challenges:

• Of paramount importance is the reconstruction and recovery from the damages of war. Hundreds of thousands of persons were killed or wounded and about 3.4 million of the prewar population is displaced, either domestically or abroad. Refugees need to be resettled and soldiers demobilized. Also, bridges, roads, housing, and water and sewerage facilities need to be repaired and public services restored. This will require a massive and well-coordinated assistance effort to prevent waste and delays.

• Second, government institutions for macroeconomic management must be developed. Institutions at all levels of government need to be designed and established according to the blueprints laid out in the Dayton-Paris Agreement. Some institutions already exist or can be easily re-created, while others will have to be created from scratch.

• Third, there is the unfinished transition to a market economy. The war interrupted the process of economic transformation that had already begun elsewhere in Central and Eastern Europe and in other parts of the former Yugoslavia. It is important to complete this process in order to form the basis for sustained growth.

In the sections that follow each of these challenges is addressed in turn.

Box 1.4 Principal elements of the Dayton-Paris Peace Agreement

Constitutional aspects. Bosnia and Herzegovina is a single sovereign State consisting of two Entities, the Federation of Bosnia and Herzegovina and the Serb Republic. The parties have agreed to a Constitution that calls for effective State institutions, including a presidency, a bicameral legislature, and a constitutional court. The country will have a central bank with a single currency.

Territorial aspects. The Federation will administer 51 percent of the country's territory. Sarajevo will be reunified within the Federation. The city will be open to all people of the country — all checkpoints will be removed and all closed bridges reopened. Gorazde will remain secure and accessible, linked to the Federation by a secure land corridor. The status of Brcko will be determined by arbitration in 1996. The Serb Republic will administer the remaining 49 percent of the country's territory.

Electoral aspects. Free and democratic elections will be held within six to nine months of the Agreement for the presidency and legislature of Bosnia and Herzegovina, for the presidency and legislature of the two Entities, and, if feasible, for local offices. All persons eighteen years or older listed on the 1991 census of Bosnia and Herzegovina are eligible to vote. Refugees and persons displaced by the conflict will have the right to vote in their original places of residence unless they choose to vote elsewhere.

War crimes tribunal. The Federal Republic of Yugoslavia, Croatia, and Bosnia and Herzegovina agree to cooperate fully with the international investigation of war crimes and violations of international humanitarian law. The new constitution obligates the authorities in both Entities to comply with the orders of the war crimes tribunal. Indicted war criminals who refuse the tribunal's orders are prohibited from holding appointed or elected office in Bosnia and Herzegovina. A sanction suspension resolution subsequently introduced by the United Nations Security Council stipulates that compliance with the tribunal's orders is an essential element of the peace agreement.

Human rights aspects. All parties in Bosnia and Herzegovina agree to respect the highest level of recognized human rights, to grant human rights monitors unrestricted access to their territory, to cooperate with the International Committee of the Red Cross in the search for missing persons, and to release all persons detained during the conflict. A human rights commission has been created, with a human rights ombudsman who has the authority to investigate and act on human rights violations.

Military aspects.   The Agreement obligates the parties to withdraw their forces behind an agreed cease-fire line within thirty days and establishes demilitarized zones of separation on both sides of the line. It provides for confidence-building measures, including the withdrawal of heavy weapons and forces to barracks and restrictions on military deployments. The Agreement provides for the creation of a peace implementation force under the command of NATO and with a grant of authority from the United Nations. The force will monitor and enforce compliance with the military aspects of the settlement, including the cease-fire and separation of forces. All parties are committed to full cooperation with the force, which will have unimpeded freedom of movement in Bosnia and Herzegovina.

Police aspects. The Agreement includes a request by the parties to the United Nations to establish an International Police Task Force to train and advise local law enforcement personnel and monitor law enforcement activities, facilities, and proceedings.

Civilian aspects. The Agreement includes a request for the designation of a High Representative to facilitate civilian aspects of implementation of the Peace Agreement, such as providing humanitarian aid, facilitating economic reconstruction, promoting human rights, and holding free elections. The High Representative will chair a Joint Civilian Commission (JCC) that includes political representatives of the parties, the implementation forces' commander, and representatives of civilian organizations.

Public Corporations. The Agreement mandates the establishment of "a Commission on Public Corporations to examine establishing Bosnia and Herzegovina Public Corporations to operate joint public facilities, such as those for the operation of utility, energy, postal and communication facilities for the benefit of both Entities. The Commission shall examine in particular the appropriate internal structure for such Corporations and conditions to ensure their successful, permanent operations".

II. TOWARD RECONSTRUCTION AND RECOVERY

Economic reconstruction and recovery is an urgent necessity in Bosnia and Herzegovina —per capita GDP has fallen by three-quarters, from $1900 in 1990 to $500 in 1995, and living conditions have declined drastically. Generating employment for the millions of returning refugees, displaced persons and demobilized soldiers will be on the critical path to peace and economic recovery. Experience from countries similarly afflicted by war shows that economic recovery can proceed quickly if a number of conditions are satisfied. These conditions include: (i) a stable macroeconomic environment; (ii) a transparent and enabling legal and regulatory framework, effectively enforced by effective government and other institutions and good governance at all levels; and (iii) sufficient international assistance, official and private, channeled through good organization and coordination mechanisms. Germany grew by about 30 percent in the first year after World War II; Lebanon by an astonishing 40 percent in 1992, the first full year of peace. Private investment can also play a large role if basic infrastructure and government services are restored and macroeconomic and legal frameworks are well maintained and if the threat of war is truly over. There are, of course, numerous countries that have failed to revive their economies in a postwar environment. While there are always specific political and social reasons associated with economic failure, the absence of the conditions listed above goes a long way toward explaining economic collapse in these countries. In the context of Bosnia, a major effort will be needed, *internally*, for establishing and strengthening institutions at all levels of government and ensuring good governance, establishing an enabling legal framework, and, *externally,* for securing, and making best use of, international assistance required to fund the reconstruction program.

In the initial stage of recovery, major sources of growth will have to come from reconstruction-related activities, since domestic market and export capacities are both limited. Because significant resources will be provided by donors during the initial stage of economic recovery, a key issue is the design of the aid schemes. The most important objective is to avoid any negative effects of assistance, however well intended, on domestic recovery. Particularly critical concerns include the use of local personnel and companies in reconstruction projects and the implications of the food aid for agricultural recovery. Equally important during this initial stage is the early adoption by the government authorities of a set of measures that can immediately facilitate the startup of economic activities. These include measures that promote internal (inter-Entity and intra-Entity, in the case of the Federation) and external trade and help immediately reactivate functioning productive assets. Maintaining sound macroeconomic policies in the face of a large inflow of foreign exchange presents a particular problem, and the dynamics of price and real exchange rates movement should be well understood and taken into account in policy formulation.

Measuring the Damage and Quantifying the Reconstruction Program

The war in Bosnia and Herzegovina wrought extensive human and physical devastation. The most common measures of overall damage refer to the number of lives lost and persons wounded, or to the replacement value of destroyed physical assets and infrastructure. In terms of human losses, Bosnia and Herzegovina's total population in the 1991 census was 4.39 million people. Since then about one million have left the country, while 200,000 — 300,000 have entered the State as refugees from other countries. Furthermore, some 250,000 are thought to have died or are missing. This leaves a net population in Bosnia and Herzegovina of about 3.4 million persons, or 23 percent less than in 1991 (about 2.3 million people are located in the Federation, while 1.2 million people in the Serb Republic). In terms of physical losses, the government estimates the overall damages from the war at $50 — $70 billion. The economic replacement cost of the destroyed assets is huge; according to initial World Bank staff estimates it lies in the range of $15 —$20 billion.[1]

No simple estimates of physical damages can capture the human suffering and loss of irreplaceable works of art and cultural landmarks caused by the war. Nonetheless, these estimates illustrate the magnitude of the reconstruction and reconciliation task that lies ahead. Bosnia and Herzegovina's economy must increase more than *threefold* just to regain the level of output that it once attained. No other country in Central and Eastern Europe has experienced such a massive economic collapse since World War II. The most severely afflicted transition economies have exhibited cumulative GDP declines on the order of 30 percent (Bulgaria, Romania, Slovakia) to 40 percent (Albania, Macedonia), and 50 percent (the USSR). Bosnia and Herzegovina, on the other hand, experienced a 75 percent drop in GDP.

Working with the government, the EU, and other agencies, the World Bank has identified a basic reconstruction program with an external financing requirement of $5.1 billion over three to four years. This program is based on an assessment of the critical needs to get the recovery under way. It does not pretend to restore all the infrastructure damaged during the war; doing so would cost several times more. Rather, the goal is to sufficiently jump-start the recovery process to initiate a significant flow of domestic production, jobs, and incomes that, in turn, generates domestic resources that can be channeled toward the reconstruction effort and permit the country to be gradually weaned from its dependence on foreign aid. A key issue here is the domestic absorption capacity for digesting the anticipated flow of international assistance under this program. Clearly, the better the absorptive

---

[1] Bosnia and Herzegovina had a GDP of about $8-9 billion before the war. Assuming a capital output ratio of four to five, total prewar capital stock was $30-40 billion. Since nearly half of the capital stock is estimated to have been destroyed, the damage is presumed in the range of $15-20 billion. The government's estimates of war damages include not only physical destruction, but also the capitalized value of (i) unpaid wage and pension arrears since the war began; (ii) the capitalized value of claims on the State such as frozen foreign exchange deposits lost to citizens and enterprises during the war.

capacity, the more international resources, either public or private, are likely to flow into the country.

Priorities and Organization of Reconstruction

The most important challenge for the economic recovery program will be to create employment opportunities for returning refugees, displaced persons, and demobilized soldiers. The program will focus on the reconstruction of transport, telecommunications, energy supply, and other infrastructure severely damaged by the war, without which it is not possible to restart production and trade on any significant scale, and to repair water, sewerage, and health facilities and improve the supply of food, without which there will be a continued threat to economic sufficiency and public health. Financing for this reconstruction program will have to come mostly from abroad.

Getting such a major reconstruction program started and running smoothly is a task of enormous proportions and complexity. A well-coordinated effort by the government and the donor community will be required to deploy these resources, not only for effective targeting and efficiency in the use of resources but also for maximizing the impact on domestic economic recovery. The government's first step toward effective coordination should be to establish an institutional structure that clearly defines responsibilities for each of the elements in the reconstruction program. Considerable progress has been made in setting up viable coordination mechanisms in the country since December 1995. In mid-February 1996, Bosnia and Herzegovina created a "Reconstruction Cabinet" to help manage the priority reconstruction program. This cabinet consists of some 15 members, is chaired by the State Prime Minister, and includes members from both the Federation and Serb Republic at the prime minister and senior minister level, although participation by the Serb Republic had not yet taken place by the end of March, 1996. The role of the Cabinet is to define needs and priorities for the reconstruction and establish and implement a strategy to mobilize needed resources. Similarly, the Federation established a Coordination Board and the Serb Republic a Reconstruction Agency to define the funding needs, and priorities of the reconstruction program at the Entity level. At the sectoral level, line ministries and agencies will be responsible, through the establishment of project implementation units, for the reconstruction implementation in each sector. This arrangement maintains clear responsibility for key decision-making at the State and Entity levels, yet decentralizes sectoral implementation and helps to build up institutions responsible for implementation. It should provide an effective institutional basis for internal coordination of the reconstruction program and implementation capacity.

For donors, apart from finding an effective mechanism to coordinate among themselves to maximize the impact of assistance and minimize the burden on the government, assistance also raises important domestic policy issues. Clearly, large-scale economic recovery will not take off if weak demand — resulting from low levels of domestic income and employment in the aftermath of a devastating war—persists. One clear way to increase aggregate domestic demand is to use donor money so that it maximizes the employment of domestic companies and local employees for reconstruction projects, large or small. In this respect it is fortunate that Bosnia and Herzegovina has excellent engineering and construction capacity, both for domestic and foreign projects, and that some of its main companies continued operations abroad during the war. Large projects can be designed and undertaken jointly by Bosnia and Herzegovina and foreign companies, while smaller projects should be left for local companies and employees.

Employment Generation, Resettlement of Refugees and Demobilization

There are urgent needs for employment generation as well as housing needs to accommodate millions of returning refugees, displaced persons, and demobilized soldiers. Reintegrating these groups of personnel into the economic system will enhance the country's production capacity by increasing the available pool of labor and skills. But this potential will only be realized if these groups are properly and timely reintegrated - a major challenge in the post-war environment. At the same time, the resettlement of refugees and ex-soldiers places a significant burden on scarce resources available to the government and the donor community. Any scheme designed to facilitate the return of these groups of persons should, therefore, avoid causing long-term dependency of these groups on government handouts. A particularly relevant issue with respect to demobilization of soldiers concerns the legal requirement for enterprises to take back those ex-soldiers in the enterprise from which they came, regardless of their financial and employment situation.

Microcredit and entrepreneurship support. Multi-faceted efforts will be required to address this critical issue. In addition to pursuing a policy of employing as many as possible local personnel and local companies in the reconstruction program, creative and diversified programs will be needed to address the employment imperative. Programs such as those that facilitate *micro- and small business creation* through credit extension, rural funds, technology transfer, information dissemination, and quick privatization of small and functioning assets of State enterprises via simplified mechanisms, can be of great importance for alleviating employment pressure as well as stimulating growth. In this regard, a number of initiatives have already been taken by donors in the last few months, such as those for lines of credit, rural funds, and small businesses (see companion volume for details.)

Public works. A variety of public works programs for repairing buildings for schools and clinics, and maintaining bridges, roads, streets, urban sanitation, water systems, etc. can also be initiated to help alleviate employment pressure. Well-designed public works programs can contribute significantly to the reconstruction program and at the same time, address employment generation needs. Of course, there will be limits because of lack of fiscal resources. In this regard, retraining and outplacing programs for returned refugees and demobilized soldiers can facilitate redeploying labor force. In addition, in designing schemes for demobilization, features such as lump-sum payments for housing repairs, small credit for business activities could be incorporated into the programs to help employment generation.

A donor-financed program of housing construction (and associated water supply and sites\facilities) would also help to stimulate local employment as well as help settle refugees, displaced persons, and demobilized soldiers. Such a program would help generate income and domestic demand by increasing employment to support recovery in production and distribution, and would help contain domestically financed fiscal outlays. Donor financing of housing is also attractive in that it matches a temporary program with a temporary source of income. Moreover, to the extent that financing housing in Bosnia and Herzegovina offsets the high costs associated with the housing of refugees in many EU countries, spending money on housing construction may in fact save donors money over the medium term. Of course, to reap the production- and income-generating effects of such an effort, it is absolutely essential that extensive use is made of local labor. A major source of additional financing for housing repair is private remittances expected from Bosnians living abroad.

Food Aid and Social Security

Most foreign aid to Bosnia and Herzegovina has been channeled in the form of direct government relief and handouts. This is especially true in the case of food aid. As the economic recovery begins, however, the mechanisms for distributing foreign aid should be restructured to minimize any potentially negative effects on domestic production.

Food Aid

In 1995 domestic food production increased to nearly half the total food consumed in Bosnia and Herzegovina. The country was a net importer even before the war and is not expected to become fully self-sufficient in food production in the post-war environment: since most of its territory is hilly and not suited for agricultural production, this would be an inefficient allocation of resources. Still there is significant room for expanding domestic agricultural production before Bosnia and Herzegovina runs into major productivity constraints. Moreover, the expansion of agricultural production is one area of economic activity with greatest potential for reviving very quickly. Emergency food aid programs could slow down the speed of recovery in domestic food production, to the extent that food is distributed free of charge to segments of the population that could afford to purchase locally produced food. Now that peace is at hand, the focus of aid should shift from a humanitarian toward a mainly reconstruction perspective. Programs that perform well during wars are often inappropriate during peace (see companion volume for discussion of these issues).

To mitigate any negative effects on domestic food production, alternative mechanisms for channeling food aid should be considered. First, whenever possible, donors should procure a significant share of their food aid from sources *within* Bosnia and Herzegovina, especially in sectors where the country has a proven capacity to be a reasonably competitive supplier of certain commodities, such as cereals, flour, and meat. Doing so would generate a "demand-pull" for the agricultural and agroprocessing sectors in those parts of the economy where still-intact farm assets remain idle for lack of local purchasing power. Second, food aid should be sold rather than distributed free of charge. Members of society that require aid should be supported through targeted income transfers rather than through food handouts. This measure would also mitigate the negative impact of donated food imports on domestic agricultural production while generating revenues for the government budget and, possibly, savings in the administrative costs of food aid distribution. Such a system could also improve the targeting of assistance to needy segments of the population as the social security system is reformed. Third, the quantities and types of food provided by donors should be monitored carefully and phased out as local agricultural production recovers and commercial food imports develop. Albania successfully implemented such a program during 1993-95, and a similar program could be designed and implemented in Bosnia.

A number of practical issues concerning the sale and distribution of food need to be resolved. To begin with, an identification and transfer mechanism should be established to distribute food vouchers or cash to those in need of food support, such as displaced persons, refugees, orphans, and the disabled. The social assistance network that already exists in Bosnian and Herzegovina may be suited for this purpose. However, this initiative may require an initial cash outlay by the government (possibly with donor assistance) to bring funds into circulation that permit the subsequent monetization of food aid. As food aid becomes monetized, private enterprises should engage in the procurement, distribution, and sale of food aid, while the government's role should be limited to coordination and monitoring activities. While the government authorities at the State and the Entity-levels clearly have a role in coordinating with external donors and resolving intercantonal issues in food aid distribution, local governments also need to be involved in the implementation of the programs. The process could be envisioned as follows: Donors and the government, mostly likely the local authorities acting with approval from the State and the Federation or Serb Republic governments, would auction donated food to local wholesalers. The cash proceeds from these sales would be transferred to different levels of the government, on the basis of formulae agreed to in advance, to finance targeted income support programs. Of course, the *most* efficient mechanism would be for donors to monetize food aid in world markets and make the proceeds available in the form of balance of payments support to Bosnia. A technical assistance program to develop basic procedures and the administrative capacity to ensure an efficient and transparent distribution of aid may need to be implemented in parallel with donor assistance.

Social Assistance Mechanisms

An integral component of the economic revival strategy is to efficiently deploy scarce resources to help the poor and socially disadvantaged. By 1995, about 80 percent of Bosnia and Herzegovina's population became at least partly dependent on emergency food aid for its survival. Since June 1992, this emergency assistance has been provided by government authorities in cooperation with the United Nations High Commission on Refugees and various nongovernmental organizations in the form of food packages designed to meet minimum consumption requirements. As the economy recovers, the dependency ratio should gradually decline. For example, the authorities in the Federation project that the percentage of families requiring emergency assistance will fall to about 60 percent in 1996, 40 percent in 1997, 20 percent in 1998, and less than 5 percent in 1999. Despite this rapid projected decline, a significant share of the population will continue to depend on assistance in the medium term. This means that the phasing out of in-kind emergency food aid programs, to be replaced by monetized food aid, will require the establishment of targeted cash transfer mechanisms to avoid hardship. Temporary programs are required until pension, unemployment, and social assistance systems are restarted. A first step in this direction has been taken with the establishment of an Emergency Social Fund to meet the essential consumption needs of the poorest households. This fund was established with World Bank support under an Emergency Recovery Project approved in February 1996 and now under implementation.

Promoting Trade and Reactivating Functioning Assets

Promoting Trade by Linking Payments Systems and Removing Internal Barriers

The government authorities could also adopt additional measures to stimulate economic recovery. Removing trade barriers and expanding trade possibilities would be particularly beneficial to a private sector-based economic expansion. Currently, the existence of separate payments bureaus and separate customs administrations, even within the Federation part of the country, are major barriers to the movement of goods and services. Both barriers improve cumbersome procedures and costly delays on business transactions, raising the costs of trading and impeding recovery. These institutions should be unified with the utmost speed, particularly in the Federation. Payments system unification, in particular, is part of the banking reform that will be required to improve banking services for business and is also integral to fiscal reform.

Another major concern at the present time is the continued existence of internal checkpoints across Bosnia and Herzegovina and within the Federation that inhibits free and unencumbered movements of goods and donor supplies. These internal checkpoints are supposed to be eliminated under the Dayton-Paris Agreement, but nonetheless continue to exist. Goods transported through these checkpoints are not only imposed impromptu "taxes" and fees, but also are often held up for extended periods. Strong and immediate actions are needed by all authorities at all levels involved to remove these barriers, and a monitoring and enforcement mechanism, with international support, should be established to ensure these actions taken and no new barriers established. Unification of customs and tax administration on the Federation side will immediately eliminate those internal checkpoints in the Federation (see section III).

Opening Trade Routes

Bosnia and Herzegovina is essentially landlocked. The small stretch of Adriatic coastline is not suitable for a harbor and is not connected to other transport infrastructure. The traditional route for maritime trade is through Ploce (in Croatia), and before the war, companies in Bosnia and Herzegovina invested heavily in Ploce's port facilities to serve their needs. Under the Washington Agreement, the Ploce port will be administered by the Federation for ninety-nine years and Croatia will allow the free flow of trade and people through its territory, subject only to the usual transit fees. Given the importance of Ploce to trade, it is imperative that this Agreement be implemented quickly and that a suitable ports administrator be named. Additional commerce routes from the northern and central parts of Bosnia and Herzegovina to Croatian ports need to be explored. Alternative routes would promote competition and thereby reduce transport costs.

Trade Agreements and Export Credit Cover

Bosnia and Herzegovina's access to international markets is hampered by the absence of trade agreements and the lack of any cover by export credit agencies. The signing of a free trade agreement with Croatia in 1994 is a positive step toward expanding the country's market access and should be implemented without delay. The European Union also could move to provide preferential treatment for goods from Bosnia and Herzegovina before starting the time-consuming process of working out a comprehensive trade agreement. The absence of export insurance cover is particularly damaging at this stage. Even for traditional exports, such as construction services, suppliers from Bosnia and Herzegovina cannot obtain the compliance guarantees necessary for international bidding without placing a 100 percent back-to-back deposit with a foreign bank. Regaining comprehensive export insurance coverage in OECD countries will depend on normalizing relations with other creditors. Still an interim agreement providing a minimal amount of acceptable guarantees not requiring back-to-back deposits would be highly desirable. One possible temporary solution might be for a friendly government to provide a contingent commitment that could serve as backing. Such an agreement would give more time for the design of a permanent solution to be in place once the initial reconstruction process is well under way.

Reactivating Functioning Assets

The quick privatization of still-functioning but idle assets of State enterprises (trucks, machines, sheds) could be of great help in starting a private sector-led recovery. These assets could be split off and sold through simple mechanisms by the enterprises themselves under, say, municipal supervision, similar to what has been tried in Albania, Croatia, and Russia. This effort would require moving away from any complicated privatization schemes, such as those that have been implemented in other republics of the former Yugoslavia.

The Macroeconomics of Economic Recovery

Bosnia and Herzegovina has been remarkably successful in maintaining orderly macroeconomic indicators despite the war. This was achieved partly by close integration with regions that had successfully stabilized (Croatia and to a lesser extent the Federal Republic of Yugoslavia) and partly through competent monetary stabilization. The move toward economic growth will be different from what has been observed elsewhere in Central and Eastern Europe; the impetus for growth will clearly come from the reconstruction effort, not from exports, at least for the next two to three years. Thus the macroeconomics of transition will also be different. Contrary to, say, Poland, the overriding goal should not be export competitiveness, since a large reconstruction program will in itself provide the initial impetus for growth. Not until normal infrastructure has been brought back can a switch in growth strategy be considered. The key macroeconomic challenge is likely to be the management of the large inflows that will fuel the reconstruction effort and the careful focus on removing bottlenecks in this process in order to avoid undue price pressures and delays.

Maintaining macroeconomic stability will be a key requirement for successful recovery and, if experience elsewhere in Eastern Europe is any guide, is a prerequisite to rather than an enemy of renewed growth. Two key problems are likely to emerge. The first is the threat of a reignition of inflation. The currency board arrangement being put in place for the new central bank sends a good signal that the process of institution-building will not interfere with monetary management. However, large expenditure needs and the fragile fiscal situation clearly threaten the fiscal support for the strict monetary policy envisaged under the currency board. Thus establishing a fiscal structure that allows for effective control of deficits at all levels of the government is a key priority (Issues in the design of new fiscal institutions and arrangements are discussed in section III of this report.)

The second problem concerns the management of the exchange rate in an environment of reconstruction-driven construction efforts. Experience elsewhere suggests that such activities, once the initial slack in the sector is taken up, will exert strong upward pressure on the real exchange rate because much of the demand for domestic resources will be directed toward non-tradeables. Such appreciation is not a problem in itself: as long as the reconstruction effort continues, it is simply a reflection of market realities. There are two problems, however, one of which requires urgent attention; the other will emerge some years from now.

For reasons that are clear, a currency board has been chosen as the initial exchange rate arrangement. With institution building at such an early stage, the choice for a zero-discretion policy system is understandable. However, such an approach poses several problems. First, exchange rate crises can occur even under a currency board arrangement. A currency board offers less safety than is generally thought: it is typically run against base money, which provides complete safety against exchange of the currency stock. However, the public can also withdraw deposits and attempt to change the resulting monies into foreign exchange. If that happens, the authorities have only two options if they anticipate that the flow will be too large: they can block the deposit withdrawal or refuse the exchange of money, that is, they can choose between a banking crisis or a foreign exchange crisis. Complete safety is only possible if a currency board is run against total stock of money including deposits; however, this would effectively mean a shutdown of the banking system, because the latter would not be allowed to perform any intermediation function. Since such an extreme policy is clearly out of the question, the authorities need to be aware that the currency board provides only partial protection against currency crises.

The second problem with a currency board goes almost in the opposite direction. Under this regime, not only does the central bank lose any role in monetary policy, but it also can not provide any liquidity to the banking system. In normal times, this is a positive feature. But during a banking crisis, central bank intervention is often essential. Thus a currency board increases the vulnerability of the banking system and therefore requires more supervision and stricter bank regulation to limit risk exposure.

Finally, there is the problem of how, with a fixed nominal exchange rate, the pressure for real appreciation can be accommodated. There are two options: nominal revaluation or domestic inflation in excess of foreign inflation. Nominal revaluation is easy to implement but in a sense defeats the purpose of the currency board because it reintroduces discretion in the system. Domestic inflation in excess of foreign inflation requires careful judgment on when inflation is reflecting inappropriate monetary and fiscal policies rather than a justified real exchange rate adjustment.

The same problem in reverse will emerge once the reconstruction effort nears completion or at least starts to slow down significantly. A real depreciation will then be called for, and this is even harder to achieve with a currency board. Once again, real depreciation can be brought about through inflation differentials, but the currency board is pegging the dinar to the Deutsche mark, and German inflation is low. Depreciating will require lower inflation than Germany, clearly an impossible objective.

In conclusion, large inflows of foreign exchange associated with the reconstruction program will put strong upward pressure on the real exchange rate. Prices will likely go up. That in itself is not a problem; as long as the reconstruction effort continues, this is simply a reflection of market realities. However, over time the exchange rate may become overvalued and uncompetitive. Careful judgment is therefore needed on when inflation is reflecting inappropriate monetary and fiscal policies rather than being a justified real exchange rate adjustment. Several measures can be taken to minimize the degree of real exchange rate appreciation and its adverse consequences. Most important in this regard is the elimination of domestic barriers to the free flow of goods and factor services, including labor, which in turn requires legal and administrative reform in trade management, labor markets, and the financial sector.

III. BUILDING A VIABLE STRUCTURE FOR ECONOMIC MANAGEMENT

The peace agreement devolves most governmental responsibilities and the control over revenues from the State to the constituent Entities, that is, the Federation of Bosnia and Herzegovina and the Serb Republic. The agreements on decentralized structures for the State and the Federation—the Serb Republic remains centrally organized—are designed to eliminate major sources of conflict between the ethnic or religious groups living in the country while preserving the possibility for a pluralistic, multicultural society to reemerge. However, as the failure of the former Yugoslavia demonstrates, a decentralized structure is only viable if the country's national and inter-jurisdictional links are mutually beneficial, and this requires that the institutional arrangements for macroeconomic control are maintained and institutions are sufficiently strong to fulfill key responsibilities. Building a viable structure for economic management within the framework of the peace agreement is therefore essential if Bosnia and Herzegovina is to continue on the road of reconstruction and prosperity.

This effort will involve two tasks: rapidly building a core set of State and Federation institutions, with competent staff from all groups to establish credibility for the new structures and foster cooperative behavior, and clarifying fiscal arrangements between the State and its two constituent Entities, and between the Federation and cantons, including the assignment of revenue and expenditure responsibilities across levels of government and the establishment of intergovernmental revenue redistribution mechanisms. In this regard some fundamental issues, such as those concerning the tax system, will have to be sorted out early on. A tax such as a value-added tax cannot be implemented effectively if it is not imposed and collected at the national level. To lay the background for the discussions to follow, this chapter begins with a brief review of the evolution of monetary and fiscal systems and policies in Bosnia and Herzegovina following independence in 1991, then proceeds to examine these two key challenges for building a viable structure for economic management.

Evolution of Monetary and Fiscal Management between 1992-95

The economic structure of the former Yugoslavia was characterized by a regional decentralization of its fiscal, monetary, financial, and enterprise systems. Branches of each system, such as the central bank or the payments system, were present in each of the republics that formed Yugoslavia. While these republican branches were not separate, they were independent from one another and had significant discretionary powers relative to the central, or federal government. Key personnel for these institutions were always appointed by the republican authorities.

Evolution of Monetary Policy and Institutions between 1992-95

Monetary and banking developments in the Bosniac majority area. As part of the former Yugoslavia's dinar area, Bosnia and Herzegovina was subject to the extremely lax monetary policies adopted by the Yugoslav central bank during 1989 and the early 1990s. When political independence was declared in March 1992, Bosnia and Herzegovina's Parliament adopted the same regulations that had applied before to the central and commercial banks. These regulations were in effect until January 1993, with the Sarajevo branch of the National Bank of Yugoslavia acting as the central bank. On January 15, 1993, the National Bank of Bosnia and Herzegovina (NBBH) was created as the central bank of the Republic, although its sphere of influence only comprised the Bosniac majority areas. The NBBH was given a certain degree of independence that strengthened over time. Its key responsibilities include maintaining currency stability, sufficient foreign reserves, and adequate liquidity for the economy. It is also in charge of licensing, regulating, and supervising the commercial banks and other depository institutions (nondeposit financial institutions are under the jurisdiction of the Finance Ministry). There are currently twenty-eight banks that report to the NBBH. The rapid depreciation of the dinar throughout 1993 and early 1994 led to the widespread use of the deutsche mark and the U.S. dollar, which became legal tender for all practical purposes. On August 14, 1994, the NBBH introduced a currency reform, restricting the status of legal tender to the new Bosnian dinar and, for some transactions, the deutsche mark. The new dinar was viewed as a transitional currency until peace and economic stability were restored. Political considerations would then argue for the introduction of a single national currency.

The new Bosnian dinar (BHD) is pegged to deutsche mark at a fixed exchange rate of BHD 100 deutsche mark. Commercial banks authorized to carry out foreign exchange transactions are not subject to surrender requirements on current transactions if the client has proof of having paid all tax obligations. Banks are free to operate in the currency market with their own funds. Throughout the Bosniac majority territory, the market exchange rate has been roughly in line with the official rate, except on a temporary basis in enclaves afflicted by restrictions on movement. To support this fixed exchange rate policy, the central government adopted a policy of balancing the budget on a cash basis, requiring no financing from the NBBH. Since the second half of 1994, the bank has limited the expansion of base money to whatever purchases of foreign exchange it could effect in the market. This strategy stabilized the currency and allowed an accumulation of some $74 million in gross reserves by the end of 1994.

The NBBH sets reserve requirements on dinar-denominated deposits using a system developed by the former National Bank of Yugoslavia that takes into account the liquidity of each deposit and a bank's history of credit expansion. The average required reserve ratio is currently 14 percent. Interest is paid on required bank reserves at the rate of 2.5 percent a month, rising to 3 percent for excess reserves. Banks have access to a short-term discount window for up to 80 percent of their required reserves but are charged a monthly interest rate of 10 percent. Banks also have access to NBBH resources through a selective credit facility. This facility is meant to support economic recovery with credits targeted at the food and export sectors. Through this facility commercial banks can rediscount up to one-third of new loans granted to these preferred sectors at a rate of 3 percent a month, but with a maximum spread of 1 percentage point. The demand for this selective credit facility has been extremely limited. The discount rate on selective credits, however, plays a role in controlling market interest rates, which cannot exceed the discount rate by more than 50 percent. The discount rate is adjusted to the inflation rate: it was reduced from 40 percent a month in June 1994 to 20 percent in December 1994, to 3—5 percent in June 1995. Dinar-denominated market interest rates have followed a similar decline.

Monetary and banking developments in the Croat majority area. The Bosnia dinar was never accepted as legal or practical tender in the Croat majority area. Instead, the Croatian kuna was adopted, but no separate central bank has been established. Nine new commercial banks were established in the Croat majority areas; they reported to the Ministry of Finance of the local authorities based in Mostar. Upon their establishment, these banks were for all intents and purposes part of the Croatian banking system. When the local authorities realized that net savings were flowing out of the region, they imposed tight restrictions on financial flows with the Croatian banking system. However, the payments system remained linked with the Croatian banking system. The deutsche mark, U.S. dollar, and Croatian kuna were declared legal tender, and full convertibility existed between all three currencies. Reserve requirements for commercial banks were set at 40 percent, with reserves having to be kept either with the payment bureau or in banks' own vault in cash.

Monetary and banking developments in the Serb majority area. The Serb majority area has retained strong links with the monetary system in the Federal Republic of Yugoslavia, and a central bank was established in Banja Luka, that is empowered to extend credit but not to print money. When sanctions were imposed in August 1994, the area continued to use the Yugoslav dinar as its legal tender through the issue of bank cashier's cheques that were supposed to be backed by dinar-denominated giro deposits in local banks. Since these cheques are not accepted outside the Serb majority territory, they have traded at a substantial discount; about 30 percent in the area of Pale in early February 1996. To maintain currency stability, the Serb Republic pursued extremely tight fiscal and monetary policies: fiscal budgets were balanced on a cash basis and the central bank severely limited access by commercial banks, especially in rediscounting credits to the large enterprises.

In addition to the central bank, the financial sector in the Serb Republic includes thirteen commercial banks, the postal savings system, and insurance companies. The central bank's main functions are to license and regulate commercial banks, administer the foreign exchange system, and act as the government's fiscal agent. Certain sectors, including agriculture and exporters, are eligible for selective credit at regulated interest rates. Interest subsidies are compensated directly from the central government budget and not through central bank credits or other means that could affect the money supply. Interest rates on most other types of commercial loans are freely determined. Liquidity is controlled in part through reserve requirements at a rate specified by the central bank for domestic and foreign exchange deposits. The central bank does not engage in domestic transactions with the nonfinancial, nongovernment sector.

Evolution of Fiscal Policy and Institutions between 1992-95

Following independence in 1992, Bosnia and Herzegovina inherited the former Yugoslavia's decentralized fiscal structure. This structure comprises a limited central government budget, mainly responsible for defense, administration, subsidies for State-owned banks and enterprises and supplementary funding for social services in education, health, and social transfers; a large number of extrabudgetary funds for social sector expenditures (such as pensions, health, unemployment, education, sports, and culture) and infrastructure development; and local government budgets for local administration and services. A process of fiscal centralization, meant to consolidate or eliminate most extrabudgetary funds, was initiated in the late 1980s in most of the republics of the former Yugoslavia and was planned for Bosnia and Herzegovina after independence.

The Social Accounting Office is one of the key institutions for fiscal management inherited by Bosnia and Herzegovina. This office combined payments settlement, tax and customs tariff collection, financial auditing, and holding of cash reserves for the banking system in one powerful organization. All the financial transactions of economic, social, and political entities were certified or carried out through the office. This unique position made the Social Accounting Office into an obvious choice for collecting taxes in the former Yugoslavia. The office performed all the functions of a fiscal revenue collection agency—assessment, collection, and verification of tax obligations — in an efficient manner. It also carried out the allocation of tax revenues and payroll contributions across all levels of government and for the extrabudgetary funds on the basis of legislation and government decisions, and performed basic treasury functions for all fiscal entities. Under political pressure, the office sometimes abused its position by extending credits to enterprises through the giro accounts it maintained for them, circumventing central bank control.

The Social Accounting office was in the process of being reformed when the republics of the former Yugoslavia began declaring independence. With the outbreak of war, it collapsed quickly in Bosnia and Herzegovina, along with the country's other political and economic structures. In its place, three payments bureaus developed, one for each of the three areas controlled by separate military and political forces. Since then fiscal policies and systems have evolved differently in each area, though all are based on the original Social Accounting office infrastructure.

Fiscal developments in the Bosniac majority area. The fiscal revenue base in the Bosniac majority area collapsed following the outbreak of war. The few taxes that continued to be collected were mostly raised and used by the local authorities for locally provided services. These constraints forced the Bosniac majority area government to rely heavily on inflationary financing. Until June 1994, about 90 percent of the government's expenditures were financed by credit from the central bank, resulting in hyperinflation. The stabilization program implemented in the summer of 1994 was accompanied by several structural reforms that recentralized tax collection and budget management and restored the payments system for Bosniac-controlled areas. These reforms resulted in significant revenue increases and improved expenditure control. By the time the stabilization program started, all extrabudgetary funds had been consolidated into the government budget, with the central government budget playing a predominant role in the allocation of total resources. A Payments Bureau, based on the former Social Accounting office, was established under the control of the National Bank of Bosnia and Herzegovina. A Tax Administration was established to assess tax obligations. Tax collection responsibility remained with the new Payments Bureau. A financial police force was created using former Social Accounting office staff trained in financial investigation, and an audit board was established to develop audit regulations and standards for the Bosniac majority area.

In the Bosniac area, two budgets had been prepared through the end of 1995: one in Bosnian dinars and one in deutsche marks. The deutsche mark budget was about twice the size of the dinar budget. These cash budgets were prepared on a three-month cycle. There are no budgetary procedures other than the requirement of maintaining a budgetary balance on a cash flow basis. Nonmilitary outlays account for about half of total spending; the Republican army accounts for the rest. Nonmilitary outlays mostly cover government operating costs. There are currently about 10,000 public employees, of whom about 2,000 are civil servants in the central government. The public salary scale ranges from DM 40 to 320 per month; if paid, the average salary would be about DM 196. The social benefit and transfer system is integrated as part of the budget. There are currently about 200,000 pensioners with minimum and maximum pensions of DM 5 and 30 a month and an average pension of about DM 10 — well below the minimum salary for the public sector. Like wages, pensions are not always paid. There is significant accumulation of wage and pension arrears because of lack of fiscal resources.

The main sources of revenues in foreign currency includes excise taxes, custom duties, diplomatic fees, and social security contributions and payroll taxes from abroad. In domestic currency, the main sources of revenues include the turnover (sales) tax, customs, corporate, and social security contributions and payroll taxes. An estimated 150,000 people are in the registered work force, and until recently, payroll taxes and contributions amounted to 66 percent of the gross wage and salaries, with roughly equal contributions from employees and employers. The contribution of personal income tax has almost disappeared, given the virtual nonpayment of wages.

Recent tax reforms have simplified the tax system considerably. The government introduced a corporate profit tax to replace the previous corporate income tax that, at a flat 36 percent rate, is consistent with international norms. In the past sales taxes had eight tariff types and twenty-six rates, there are now five types and five rates (26 percent, 10 percent, 6 percent, 5 percent, and 0 percent), with the high rates applied to luxury goods and the low rates to primary goods. Personal income tax rates have also been reduced. Customs duties were reformed and brought in line with rules established by the General Agreement on Tariffs and trade and the World Trade Organization. There are now only five customs tariff rates (20 percent, 15 percent, 10 percent, 5 percent, and 0 percent). The list of taxpayers includes 3,000 firms, 5,000 small businesses, and 170,000 personal income taxpayers. Of course, most of these are not currently in a position to pay taxes.

The revenue collection force includes personnel for tax administration, personnel for customs tariff collection, and the financial police. In the past, following the practice of the former Yugoslavia, taxes were collected through the payments system of the Social Accounting office and no independent tax administration institution existed. Now a new Payments Bureau has been set up that is responsible for collecting taxes for the government. The government budget pays the salaries for customs personnel and the financial police directly, while the Payments Bureau covers its own operating costs, including personnel expenditures. Financial incentives are given for tax auditors in the financial police force to identify tax evasion.

Tax revenues are distributed among the central authorities in the Bosniac area, the districts, and the municipalities with shares that vary by tax, except for custom revenues that are retained fully by the central government budget (see below). Municipalities have limited taxing powers and are empowered only to impose the agricultural tax, the individual owners tax, and the communal tax. Furthermore, the tax revenue of a locality from its own taxes cannot exceed 10 percent of its total revenues.

Customs administration and customs revenue allocation have been adversely affected by the existence of dual authorities within the Federation. Until an early 1995 agreement under which customs revenues are allocated to each party within the Federation based on the final destination of the imports, the authorities in the Croat majority area collected and retained customs tariff revenues (and possibly other taxes). This approach implied that either the custom duties had to be collected more than once or that the Bosniac authorities completely forewent the custom revenues. With the new agreement, this situation has been avoided, but technical difficulties in implementing this agreement created loopholes for customs tariff collection and continue to cause major difficulties for importers.

Fiscal developments in the Croat majority areas. A separate fiscal system emerged in the Croat majority areas as a consequence of the fighting between Bosnian Croats and Bosniacs in 1993—94. Its Social Security Accounting Office system, customs administration, tax administration, and budget are in many ways similar to the system in place in the Bosniac majority territory. The main difference between the two systems is that the Croat system still maintains three extrabudgetary funds for pensions, health, and unemployment, with certain wage contributions and taxes earmarked for these funds (these were integrated into the budget during the war in the Bosniac area.)

The budget is in Croatian kuna and is compiled and executed every three months. The budget's main sources of revenue include customs, excise, and sales taxes and to a much lesser extent payroll, personal income, and company income taxes. In 1995, estimated total revenue for the budget reached about DM 150 million. In addition, the estimated total revenue for the three extrabudgetary funds was DM 120 million. There is also a separate fund that draws resources from overseas for military expenses. The size of this fund is unknown. A monthly withdrawal of 100 million kuna (about DM 30 million) from this fund has been reported.

The budget covers administration, supplementary financing for the military, supplementary funding for social transfers (such as child care), and subsidies to public enterprises in the transport, telecommunications, and energy sectors. Expenditures are kept in line with available revenue by adjusting the amount of transfers made by the budget to the military budget (which is separate). The extrabudgetary funds for pension, health, and unemployment are more or less balanced, and the authorities consider this situation sustainable. There are about 52,000 pensioners, each paid about DM 60 a month, and 3,160 users of health funds (clinics and hospitals as well as doctors and nurses). There are 105 staff in each of these two funds, and their salaries are covered by the funds. In 1995 the health fund was estimated to have spent DM 58 million, and the pension fund, DM 57 million. The unemployment fund is rather small, with total 1995 expenditure estimated at just DM 4.5 million, less than 1 percent of the area's GDP.

A customs administration for Bosnia and Herzegovina was established three years ago. It is headquartered in Mostar and has three customs offices, ten external (border) checkpoints, and eleven internal checkpoints. It has 260 employees, with monthly wages of DM 350 — DM 420. The operating cost of the customs administration has been about 4 percent of total customs revenues (tariff and excise collection). The tax administration is also headquartered in Mostar. It has twenty-eight branches throughout the territory with 326 employees and an average monthly wage of DM 350. While both the customs administration and tax administration are responsible for assessing tax and customs obligations, the Social Accounting Office is responsible for actually collecting the taxes due.

Harmonization and unification of fiscal systems within the Federation. The fiscal systems in the two parts of the Federation were quite similar even before the Washington Agreement, having both been part of the Social Accounting Office system. After the Agreement, a number of measures were taken to promote further integration of the two systems. The system's import regimes were unified in March 1995 following the adoption by the Federation Assembly of a Customs and Customs Tariff Law along the lines of the Croatian import regime. Further, the collection of revenues is closely coordinated between the two customs administrations. The laws and regulations on sales taxes, excise taxes, and direct taxes are also mostly harmonized. In October 1995, the Federation government signed a trade agreement with Croatia that will extend to the entire Federation the existing bilateral trade arrangements between the Croat majority areas and Croatia, involving a flat tariff of 1 percent on goods accompanied by a certificate of origin issued by local chambers of commerce. A consolidated picture of the 1995 Federation budget is shown in table 3.1.

Table 3.1 Consolidated Federation Government revenues, 1995 (in millions of DM)				
	Bosniac Area	Croat Area	Federation	(Percent of GDP)
Total revenues	378	590	968	30
Tax revenues	301	448	749	23
Customs duties	44	51	95	3
Excise taxes	51	60	111	3
Sales taxes	126	292	418	13
Corporate profits tax	8	14	22	1
Personal income tax	21	22	43	1
Self employment tax	--	3	3	0
Franchise tax	--	2	2	0
Property tax	5	1	6	0
Transactions tax	--	1	1	0
Tax on royalties/patents	--	0	0	0
Other taxes and fees	46	2	48	2
Contributions/payroll	77	142	219	7
Pension	37	60	97	3
Health	36	55	91	3
Education	--	23	23	1
Unemployment	4	4	8	0

Note: 1995 GDP in Federation is estimated as DM 3,190 million.
"—" means not applicable.

Fiscal policy in the Serb Republic. The fiscal policies and institutions in the Serb Republic are quite similar to those in the two areas of the Federation. A single budget denominated in Yugoslav dinars is prepared at the central level (also on a quarterly basis), and covers the central government, social funds, military expenditures, and municipalities. Municipalities share in tax revenue under sharing formulas established by Parliament. Excise and sales taxes are the main source of public revenues. The payments bureau, also modeled on the Social Accounting Office, transfers tax revenues directly to municipal accounts according to the sharing formulas. As in the Croat majority territory, there are separate pension, health, and unemployment funds. Tax collection and administration are the responsibility of the Ministry of Finance, which also controls the financial police.

There are about 170,000 pensioners, while the number of formal sector employees is only around 30,000. The health fund has been rendered practically irrelevant in light of the current health sector policy of universal and free coverage independent of insurance. Even so, most health care resources appear to consist of donations from Médecins Sans Frontières (Doctors Without Borders) or the Red Cross. The unemployment fund, which was set up for private sector employees, has few beneficiaries since the vast majority of employment is concentrated in the public sector, including the military. According to government officials, pensions and public salaries have been paid regularly throughout the war, albeit often at very low levels.

Overall assessment of fiscal and monetary developments. The authorities in all three areas of Bosnia and Herzegovina have worked toward establishing basic institutional and policy frameworks. Given the difficult economic conditions in recent years and the limited institutional infrastructure, the achievement of stability since mid-1994 is remarkable. But as the authorities in each area have recognized, these achievements are fragile, and much more needs to be done to lay a firm foundation for macroeconomic stability. This requires, first, the rapid establishment or consolidation of a core set of macroeconomic institutions at both the State and Entity levels and, second, clarification and organization of a new fiscal structure for the State, in particular the Federation. A unified—and not necessarily centralized—decision making authority for key economic policies across the State and the Federation is particularly desirable if further progress is to be made on the macroeconomic front.

Building Government Institutions within the Framework of the Dayton-Paris Agreement

For Bosnia and Herzegovina to emerge as a pluralistic, multi-religious country, it is crucial that viable institutional arrangements for economic control be established at the State and Entity levels. The peace agreement assigned to the State level all those responsibilities needed for Bosnia and Herzegovina to be recognized internationally as one State. It also called for accelerating the building of the Federation as one of the two functioning Entities within Bosnia and Herzegovina. In late 1995 specific steps were also agreed on to strengthen the Federation. These include the clear separation of the governments of the Federation and of the State of Bosnia and Herzegovina, the formation of cantons as the main political subunits of the Federation, and the establishment of central economic institutions in the Federation, to include a single, unified Federal Customs Administration, a single Federal Tax

Administration, a unified payments system, and a common region for bank licensing and supervision. The separation of governments occurred in late January 1996 with the establishment of separate cabinet ministries and ministers for all State-level and Federation-level ministries, but the cantons and central economic institutions of the Federation have yet to be established. Commitment to follow through with these institution-building measures was reconfirmed by the parties to the Dayton-Paris Agreement at the Rome meeting of February 18, 1996.

Key Institutional Arrangements at the State Level

Establishing a State-level central bank. Aside from a Parliament, the presidency, and a small administration focusing mostly on international affairs, the key economic institution to be established at the State level is a new central bank. The Constitution provides considerable guidance on how the central bank would function. It indicates that it will be the only authority for monetary policy and for issuing currency in Bosnia and Herzegovina, that it will function as a currency board during its first six years, and that during those six years, its governor will be recommended to the presidency by the management of the International Monetary Fund, and will not be a citizen of Bosnia and Herzegovina or any neighboring State.

The adoption of a currency board means that there will be a fixed exchange rate between the new domestic currency and the deutsche mark and that the central bank will only issue currency in exchange for increases in foreign exchange reserves. As a currency board, the central bank will not provide credit to any part of the economy, public or private. This arrangement will allow the country to maintain economic stability while relying on simple rules for exchange rate and monetary policy. If the central bank had discretion over the exchange rate or over the extension of credit, there would be a need for frequent decisions on matters of great political and economic sensitivity to both Entities. Such decisions could be divisive and lead to undesired outcomes, as the experience with discretionary monetary policies in the former Yugoslavia has shown.

The new central bank will play an important role in improving economic conditions in Bosnia and Herzegovina by promoting confidence in the ability to maintain economic stability. Most important, a common currency will facilitate trade and financial flows throughout the country, creating opportunities for growth and employment. Since the new central bank will not extend credit under the currency board mechanism, other economic policies must be consistent with this arrangement. In particular, the central bank will be obliged to buy or sell domestic currency freely on demand at the official exchange rate, the bank cannot extend credit to commercial banks to finance their lending operations, and the government budgets at all levels cannot make use of central bank credit. Governments at all levels will not be able to spend more than they raise in taxes or external financing. This is basically the same fiscal policy that is being implemented in the Federation and the Serb Republic—which provides a good starting point for the creation of the new central bank.

Banking supervision. For the same reason that maintaining two banking authorities within the Federation would be inefficient and would potentially lead to distortions, the existence of separate supervision agencies within each Entity also entails inefficiencies. It would, therefore, be best to form a single banking agency at the State level, providing a uniform set of rules and regulations for all banks operating within Bosnia and Herzegovina. This could be achieved either by designating this function to the State central bank or by establishing a new separate State-level banking supervision agency.

Linking payments systems. Similarly, payments systems between the two Entities should be linked. Initially, the payments bureau systems of the Federation and Serb Republic could be linked in the way the payments bureaus of the two areas of the Federation were linked in November 1995. This would allow direct transactions (in deutsche marks) to be effected between the Federation and the Serb Republic without recourse to third parties. Over time, full linkage and integration of the two systems could be designed and implemented. The intention to set up a joint working group for this purpose, as announced recently after discussions between the officials of the State government and the officials of the Serb Republic, is an encouraging step in the right direction.

Key parameters of a settlement mechanism between the Federation and the Serb Republic would include deciding on (i) the settlement currency, and (ii) settlement frequency. Guiding principles for negotiations of an agreement would presumably include commonality of currency across Entities and the need for transparency and confidence building. The deutsche mark is the only candidate for a settlement currency within these parameters, and a settlement frequency that would effectively prohibit the accumulation of large net balances would be desirable, possibly two or three times every week. Net balances could be settled through correspondent accounts abroad or physically, in line with the Federation settlement mechanism. If the second approach is chosen, the ideal settlement site would likely be in the northern part of the country near Banja Luka and Tuzla. The establishment of a settlement mechanism would be followed by the integration of the payments systems existing in the two Entities and the creation of a payments system for the State of Bosnia and Herzegovina.

Customs and trade policy. Preliminary agreement has also been reached on establishing a working group on customs systems between the two Entities. The aim of the working group is to seek understanding and agreement on a common open trade regime without quantitative restrictions and to reduce the divergence of tariff rates. In this context the discrepancies between the trade regime of the Federation and that of the Serb Republic will have to be addressed. Common customs procedures will have to be adopted between the two Entities as the Serb Republic establishes its customs checkpoints on the country's eastern borders.

Key Institutions in the Federation

Formation of Federation Customs and Tax Administrations. Although trade within the Federation is not legally subject to tariffs or quantitative restrictions, double taxation does in practice take place as each of the existing customs administrations seeks to recover revenues from goods sold in areas under its control but originally imported into the other part of the Federation. To eliminate this inter-Federation trade barrier and create a viable and visibly unified Federal government, it is essential that a single fiscal system for the Federation be put in place. The most important and urgently needed step in this regard is the formation of a unified Federation Customs Administration and Federation Tax Administration. Creating these institutions will require:

- Establishing headquarters and naming directors for both agencies.

- Eliminating internal borders within the Federation. All customs duties and related excise taxes are to be levied by the external Federation Customs Administration, while domestic taxes are to be collected by the Federation Tax Administration.

- Channeling tax and customs revenues to Federation government accounts, rather than the current practice of channeling those funds to separate accounts.

- Appointing an international observer and audit team as an interim measure to ensure that the new procedures of the unified Federation Customs Administration are being properly observed.

- Merging financial police with the Federation Customs and Tax Administrations. While the enforcement branch of the Payments Bureau was transformed into a financial police force in 1995, it still retains a separate identity from the customs and tax authorities, which also perform compliance work. The financial police should be merged with these two institutions as an auditing Entity.

Substantial progress has been made in implementing several of these steps: a director and deputy director of the Federal Customs Administration were appointed in March 1996, and a work program is under way to unify customs administrations and remove internal borders. In addition to these initial steps, the tax and customs administrations need to be restructured with a new set of border points and customs houses, endowed with properly trained professional staff, and equipped with modern data processing and other equipment. Assistance in this effort is being provided by various international organizations, including the International Monetary Fund, the World Bank, the European Union, and the World Customs Organization.

Unification of the payments systems. Until recently there were *no* linkages between the banking and payments systems in the two areas of the Federation. All transactions between them took place indirectly, in deutsche marks channeled through foreign banks located in foreign countries. Initial linkages were established in November 1995, making it possible to effect transactions directly between the two areas. However, full unification of the systems is necessary to complement the unification of the tax and customs administrations and to help establish a unified financial system in the Federation and should be soon completed. Key steps in the next few months include appointment of the director, deputy director, and senior staff of a unified Federal Payments Bureau, development of plans for the harmonization of procedures in all branches. Modernization of equipment is also needed and will be an ongoing process.

Establishment of a Federation Banking Agency. The licensing of banks and banking sector regulations is currently carried out by the National Bank in the Bosniac majority part of the Federation and by the local administration in the Bosnian Croat majority part of the Federation. A single Federation Banking Agency is needed to provide the basis for uniform bank licensing and regulatory standards throughout the Federation and to permit participation on an equal basis in domestic and international transactions of banks in both areas of the Federation. Draft legislation to reform banking sector regulations and establish a Federation Banking Agency has been prepared with the support of the International Monetary Fund, the World Bank, and the U.S. Agency for International Development. The legislation needs to be finalized by the authorities and submitted to Parliament.

Establishment of cantonal governments. The formation of cantons as political subunits within the Federation is a key element of the peace agreement. The establishment of such governments, however, first requires that agreement be reached on the boundaries of each of the cantons to be established. In mid-March, the Federation government indicated that the main political parties had reached agreement on the map of the different cantons. Appropriate legislation reflecting that agreement needs to be drafted and approved by the Federation Parliament.

Key Institutions in the Serb Republic

Since the Serb Republic has maintained a unitary structure and has already had central institutions, the key task is to adapt the function of these institutions toward serving a market-oriented economy, which the authorities have stated as one of their key objectives. However, a Banking Supervision Agency will need to be established separately once the central banking function is taken over at the State level. Needless to say, it will be important to have consistent and harmonized rules and regulations concerning banking supervision in both Entities. To this end, guidelines for banking supervision could be issued at the State level once the new State central bank is established. In the longer term, at least part of the supervision functions could also be taken over by the State central bank (see Section IV).

Financing the Startup of New Government Institutions in the Federation

The establishment of the key State and federal institutions involves significant upfront costs. Currently, wage payments for civil servants vary widely, with employees in Bosniac majority areas receiving much lower salaries than those in Croat majority areas. While the key State and federal institutions may initially be set up on a small scale, they require staff of high professional quality. A further requirement is that staff composition should reflect the composition of the population throughout the State and Federation territory. These structural considerations are essential for the viability of the institutions. They imply that wages for comparable positions must be equalized and raised to sufficient levels. One possibility is to fund base salaries at the State and Entity levels based on uniform (State-wide and Entity-wide) scales. These base salaries could be supplemented at each level using local resources (for example, topping up of base salaries by the cantons for civil servants at the State or Federation levels). In addition, the need to adequately equip these institutions implies significant first-year operating costs. Donor funding should be identified to cover financing for these outlays. Similar principles will apply after the elections when the State-level institutions will need to be attractive to employing staff from all parts of the country.

Toward a Viable Fiscal Structure

The Peace Agreement is clear about the structure of the monetary institution but is much more ambiguous about the fiscal structures. Under the agreement, the State revenue will come from contributions from the Federation (two-thirds) and the Serb Republic (one-third), to be financed from customs revenues collected by the two Entities (initially, the State would not have any direct tax revenues). The agreement calls for a rapid merger between the separate Croat and Bosniac institutions within the Federation and at the same time confirms the Federation Constitution, which gives significant fiscal autonomy to the cantons and municipalities. The Constitution assigns the responsibility for macroeconomic management to the Federation government, and gives customs revenues and excise tax revenues to the Federation government on an exclusive basis. However, a detailed distribution of taxing and expenditure responsibilities has not been spelled out and is subject to ongoing political and legislative discussion. This ambiguity raises important questions about the assignment of expenditure and revenue responsibilities across different levels of government and the question of intergovernmental fiscal redistribution. These questions must be satisfactorily dealt with in designing the new fiscal structure so that it functions efficiently without reigniting a major source of economic and political conflict.

Fiscal Structure at the State Level

The division of fiscal responsibility between the State and its two constituent Entities was outlined in the Dayton-Paris Agreement. However, many details and mechanisms have yet to be concretized. Under the framework, an asymmetrical fiscal arrangement for the State will emerge. On the Federation side, there will be a fairly decentralized tax and fiscal system with significant taxing and spending powers devolved to the cantons, with the Federation government responsible mainly for areas that have Federation-wide implications, such as defense and trade. On the Serb Republic side, a more centralized fiscal system, similar to the current structure, will continue.

Since taxing power will reside with the two constituent Entities of the State, consistency and coordination on tax policy and tax administration is a major issue. Some taxes, such as value-added tax, cannot be imposed at the subnational level unless internal borders are imposed, which is clearly not advisable. Likewise, customs administrations and policies must be consistent and coordinated in order to provide uniformity in protection and undistorted customs revenue collection. Otherwise, internal borders would have to be established as well.

Under the peace agreement, the State government's responsibilities will be significant but limited, since defense and social transfers are not included in the State government's list of constitutionally mandated responsibilities. The State government's budget will be small, financing mostly the operating costs of the State administration, including embassies and representations abroad. The budget will be financed entirely by contributions from the state's two Entities: the Bosniac-Croat Federation (two-thirds) and the Serb Republic (one-third), drawing from the customs revenues in each Entity. Such a system clearly runs the risk of vulnerability to the transfer from below not being forthcoming. The peace agreement provides that in the future, subject to the approval of the State Parliament, the State will be able to impose its own taxes.

Since the State is the internationally recognized Entity and international relations belong to the domain of the State government, foreign borrowing and foreign debt service should be coordinated at the State level. Both Entities also have foreign borrowing authority under the Constitution (see below). However, financing for debt service, under the initial design of the peace agreement, will have to come from additional contributions from the State's constituent Entities.

Size of Government. An important fiscal issue concerning the whole of Bosnia and Herzegovina is the size and scope of the government relative to the overall economy. The war reduced the taxing capacity of the government and concentrated most expenditures on military affairs. With the end of the war, the reduction in military spending will increase the scope for expenditures in social services and infrastructure. However, care should be taken not to revert to the high levels of taxation that characterized the former Yugoslavia. In particular, special attention should be given to addressing social security commitments. Government budgets simply cannot be burdened with social transfers based on the old formulas. In the near term, anticipated shortfalls in meeting minimum social needs should be financed with donor contributions to the social funds for pensions and social assistance. In the medium term, the authorities should try to achieve self-sufficiency for social security on the basis of the payroll tax and through pension reforms in areas such as eligibility, coverage, replacement ratio, and so on. In the longer term, a self-supporting social security system should be based on individual accounts rather than the current pay-as-you-go system. Reforms of other social expenditure may also be needed to reduce the size of the government, including severance payments, health benefits, and so on (see section IV).

Public Sector Borrowing. Prudence in domestic and external borrowing by the State government should be accompanied by a similar requirement of other levels of government. Direct borrowing by Entity and local governments from the future State central bank should be prohibited. All foreign borrowing should be coordinated by the State government or by State legislation that specifies caps on borrowing or requires authorization by the central authority for each borrowing, or both.

Fiscal Structure for the Federation

Development of a viable fiscal structure is key to the functioning of the Federation because of the current lack of clear rules and de facto division of the system into the two areas. A new fiscal structure should aim at having a small but strong Federation government and canton administrations with enough fiscal discretion and powers to accommodate the heterogeneity of the Federation. A highly centralized federal government is neither politically feasible nor economically desirable but powerful cantons at the expense of the Federation government run the risk of political disintegration or high coordination costs. The Federation government should therefore focus on activities that display significant economies of scale, and/or require substantial coordination or high uniformity. Cantons and municipalities should receive expenditures whose benefits are local and for which intercantonal coordination is minimal. Most social services and many public services fall into this category.

Options for Assigning Expenditure Functions and Revenue in the Federation

The allocation of expenditures by level of government will serve as the basis for the assignment of taxing powers. Here it is important to differentiate between the level of government that imposes the tax and undertakes its collection and administration and the level of government that actually receives the tax revenue. In other words local taxes (cantonal taxes) need not be locally administered, and federally imposed and collected taxes can be—and, in other countries often are—shared with other levels. There are thus several options for organizing the revenue system and tax administration and allocating tax revenues:

(a)   *A Centralized Approach*. Under this approach, all or most taxes (including major taxes such as the value-added tax, when introduced, the corporate income tax, and customs duties, which are best suited to a unified design) could be collected by the Federal Tax Administration. Since revenues from these taxes would exceed federally assigned spending responsibilities, the system would have to distribute some of these resources back to the cantons. Redistribution could be done by sharing some of the taxes collected by the Federation Tax Administration in an agreed fashion (there does not appear to be much support for introducing equalizing transfers into federal finances at this stage).

This approach concentrates tax policy and tax administration at the federal level and is relatively flexible in the channeling of revenues, since any sharing proportions can be used. The allocation of tax shares will determine the size of the revenues at each level of government.[2] Fears that the revenues will not be transferred to the cantons (or to the Entities if this approach were to be taken State-wide) can be addressed by constitutional or legal provisions. A tax administration staff drawn from the various regions of the Federation would also help. From a tax design and administration perspective, it is important that the major taxes (such as customs and corporate taxes, and eventually the value-added tax) *have a national uniform base*. These taxes should also be collected by the center because this facilitates collection and enforcement.

(b)   A Decentralized approach is to give most major taxing powers to the cantons and to have taxes collected at the cantonal level by cantonal tax administration authorities, which will then transfer resources ("contributions") upwards to the federal budget, as needed, to cover the cost of the Federal administration if the Federal budget needs more than the already assigned customs and excise revenue. Under this approach, the cantons will "own" the revenues (with the exception of customs). The transfer of resources to the Federation can be based on yearly or multiyear agreements, which can also include earmarking tax revenues for the Federal level. This arrangement makes the Federal government vulnerable to changing politics in local governments and subjects the Federal budget to large uncertainty, in the event that its requirements go beyond customs revenues. Moreover, allowing cantons to levy taxes could imply significant differences in tax rates and tax bases across cantons which, in the case of the corporate income tax and value-added tax, would lead to a "tax jungle" impeding domestic growth and trade. In Germany, where taxes are collected by the State (Lander) authorities on behalf of the Federal government, tax policy and design of major taxes remains

---

[2]   The smaller the volume of revenues allocated to the subnational level, the greater is the fiscal power of the central budget (Federation in this case). An advantage of this approach is that it gives the central budget the strongest capability to support macroeconomic stabilization policies. Also, decisions on allocating expenditure rights can be postponed until the administrative capacity of the cantons and municipalities increases. This advantage has to be weighed against its negative effects on the willingness of parties to participate in the Federation.

with the Federal government. While "politics" may argue for delegation of tax design and administration to the cantons, such an approach is very complicated to administer and may introduce too much uncertainty into federal fiscal planning. In other words, this degree of cantonal autonomy would be incurred at a high cost for the Federation as a whole.

(c)   An intermediate approach is to designate key taxes (such as customs and excise taxes) as Federal and to maintain a unified Federation (and ultimately State)-wide approach to tax design and tax administration for all other taxes. Revenue from these other Federally designed and collected taxes would accrue to the cantons or municipalities. This approach would give the regions greater flexibility in determining the tax burden of their populations without threatening the fiscal viability of the Federation or creating a tax jungle, and would keep administrative complications to a minimum.

Examples of these three approaches can be found in different countries. For the current situation in Bosnia - which requires continued prudent macroeconomic control as well as a fiscal system that supports growth and efficiency but allows for significant decentralization - it seems best to move in the direction of the third approach. In this way local governments would have substantial fiscal revenues and responsibilities of their own, while the Federal authorities would be given sufficient fiscal powers to support appropriate stabilization policies, coordinated at the State level (fiscal policies in the Serb Republic would similarly need to be supportive of stabilization policies of the State).

Whichever system is chosen, some poorer cantons will find that they cannot finance themselves adequately on the basis of assigned taxes, and additional resources may be required. While in its initial years the Federation budget may not be able to take on the burden of equalization, over the medium term some tools for equalization must be developed.

While the Federal Constitution assigns responsibilities across the levels of government, detailed expenditure allocations have yet to be made concrete. It is advisable that expenditure assignments be determined before proceeding too far in concretely assigning taxes to lower levels because tax assignments may be hard to change at a later stage. It is also advisable that tax administration of the key taxes needing a uniform design be centralized at the Federal level; purely local and cantonal taxes can be collected at those levels.

Efficient assignment of expenditure responsibilities

Four criteria are recommended for determining the optimal assignment of public functions to different levels of government: the potential for economies of scale, the existence of interregional spillovers, variation in preferences, and the desire for equalization and tolerance for cross-subsidies. There are tradeoffs among these criteria. The Federation Constitution has already assigned several functions to the Federation, including defense, federal police, justice, and customs administration. It would be reasonable to assign additional functions to the Federation, including telecommunications, university education, basic medical care, intercanton transport, environmental control, and part of social welfare. A recommended assignment of functions within the Federation based on such tradeoff considerations is shown in table 3.2.

Table 3.2 Assignment of public functions for the Federation		
Category	Type of service	Level of government
Health care	Primary	Municipality
	Secondary (hospitals, curative)	Canton
	Tertiary (medical research)	Federation
Education	Primary	Municipality
	Secondary	Canton/municipality
	University	Federation
Transportation	Roads and highways—intracity	Municipality
	Roads and highways—intercity	Canton
	Airports	Federation
	Public transportation—intracity	Municipality
	Public transportation—intercity	Canton
	Private transportation, taxis	Federation
Environmental	Air and water pollution	Canton
	Water and forestry	Federation/State[a]
Housing	All	Canton
Solid waste, fire protection	All	Municipality/canton
Water and sewerage	All	Municipality/canton
Land use and zoning	All	Municipality
Licensing and regulation	All	Canton
Cultural Policy	All	Canton
Tourism	All	Canton
Social Welfare	All	Canton/federation
Telecommunications	All	Federation/State[a]

[a] Some of these spending areas may at a later stage of reintegration come under the framework of the State as a whole, and involve both Entities.

Efficient assignment of fiscal revenues

Neither the State Constitution nor the Peace Agreement addresses the assignment of tax responsibilities. The only specific reference is contained in the Federation Constitution, which assigns customs duties and excise tax revenues to the Federation. This leaves room for many assignment options in building the new tax system. As a rule, canton and municipal revenues should be based on a combination of assigned revenue instruments and grants, with the goal of ensuring vertical equity—meaning that each level of government should have sufficient revenue capacity to fund the services for which it is responsible. Furthermore, tax and grant assignments must be made with an eye on both the funding of current service levels as well as future service needs. That is, revenue buoyancy must be carefully considered when assignments are made. Each level of government—the Federation, cantons, and municipalities—must have sufficiently buoyant revenue sources to provide the revenues needed to pay for the delivery of services over time.

In considering the assignment of taxes among different levels of government, it is also important to differentiate among the separate steps of the taxation process. These include collecting, auditing, and enforcement, referred to collectively as tax administration; definition of tax bases; setting of tax rates; and tax ownership. The level of government in charge of collecting a tax need not be the same level that defined the tax base, set the tax rate, or owns the tax revenues. In fact, it is recommended that for the most important taxes, definition of tax base, setting of the tax rate, and undertaking of tax collection *all* be done at the Federation level. In addition, customs tax and excises should be exclusively owned by the Federation government, while the personal income tax, corporate income tax, and value-added tax could be shared between the Federation government and cantons (table 3.3). These assignments should not be expected to remain in place indefinitely, given that demands for service delivery change and tax revenues evolve over time. Still, any assignment of taxes should last for a reasonable period of time to ensure predictability over revenue flows. The assignment of taxes, therefore, should be reviewed over the medium term. Key features of the proposed assignment are:

- Assignment of *customs* and *excise revenues* to the Federation and *sales tax revenues* to the cantons and municipalities. These assignments have already been made for 1996, and are consistent with the principles described earlier. Over time, however, the importance of customs as a source of revenue can be expected to decline. To compensate for the resulting imbalance, it is important to identify other revenue sources to be shared between the Federation and cantons. Personal and corporate income taxes could serve this balancing role. Although they do not currently generate significant resources, this is expected to change once economic activity picks up and tax enforcement is tightened.

- *Real estate taxes, automobile licensing fees,* and *surcharges* on income and sales taxes should be assigned to cantons and municipalities. Local excise taxes can be allowed either as a surcharge on Federation excises or as individual taxes in their own right. Municipalities should also have the authority to introduce additional taxes within parameters set by Federation legislation. A mechanism needs to be established in the court system for resolving disputes between levels of government.

Table 3.3

Summary of recommended tax assignments for the Federation

Tax type	Tax administration	Tax base	Tax rate	Revenue ownership
Customs	Federal level	Federal legislation	Federal legislation	Federation or Republic
Excise	Federal level	Federal legislation	Federal legislation; surcharges set by cantonal or municipal assemblies.	Federation. Cantons or municipalities may impose retail-level taxes.
Personal income	Federal or canton level	Federal legislation	Basic rate set by Federal legislation; surcharges set at cantonal level.	Shared by the Federation, cantons, and municipalities.
Corporate income	Federal level	Federal legislation	Federal legislation	Shared by the Federation, cantons, and municipalities.
Sales tax (retail level)	Federal level; feasible but complicated at the canton level	Federal legislation	Federal legislation; surcharges set at cantonal level.	Cantons and municipalities.
Property tax	Municipal level	Federal legislation	Municipal level	Municipal level
Real estate transfers	Municipal level	Federal legislation	Municipal assemblies	Municipal level
Motor vehicle	Municipal level	Federal legislation	Cantonal level	Cantons and municipalities
Social security contributions	Federal level	Federal legislation	Federal legislation	Funds
User fees-- Social services	Service-providing agency	Cantonal legislation	Cantonal or municipal providers	Service-providing agencies
Utilities	Utility company	Regulatory framework	Utility company, subject to regulatory oversight.	Utility company
Value-added tax	Federal level	Federal legislation	Federal legislation	Shared between Federation and cantons.

The eventual introduction of a *value-added tax* (VAT) will require rethinking tax assignments. By design, the VAT would replace, at least partly, existing excise and sales taxes. If this happens, it may be necessary to share VAT revenues between cantons and the Federation, depending on both the future performance of the income tax and the impact of the VAT on excise and sales tax revenues. As mentioned earlier, the VAT should ideally be imposed at the national level.

- *User fees* for utility services should be handed over to the companies providing the services. At the same time, however, these companies should be subject to corporate taxes and, eventually, the VAT. Service tariffs should be set by the companies subject to an overall legal and regulatory framework. The same applies to user fees for social services—they should be owned by the service-providing Entities and not go to a general government budget.

Intra-cantonal arrangements

The principles guiding the fiscal organization within cantons and the relationship between cantons and municipalities are similar to those guiding the relationship between the Federation and the cantons. The Federation Constitution allows cantons to structure tailored relationships with the municipalities. This flexibility will facilitate cantonal organizations in cantons with mixed communities. The relationship between the new cantonal administration and large municipalities may prove difficult if it implies a loss of fiscal power by the municipalities. This is ot now the case with the existing districts, which are much less powerful than the cantons would be.

User charges

Users of services should pay the actual cost for the provision of services to the extent possible. This principle argues for user fees wherever they are technically feasible without violating other principles of equity and equal access. The application of user charges in Bosnia and Herzegovina is currently limited to administrative and licensing fees, but such charges were more common before the war. The Constitution and Peace Agreements do not address the issue of setting fees. Nevertheless, the expansion and establishment of additional user fees is strongly recommended. In services such as water supply, sewerage, and garbage collection, it is more obvious and perhaps easier to pursue a cost recovery policy. But even in the provision of education (certainly at the tertiary level) and basic health services, some cost recovery through fees may be possible. This policy not only reduces government expenditure, therefore reducing taxing requirements, but it makes for more active citizen participation in the management of public services. Well-designed social pricing mechanisms that address the needs of the poor (such as lifeline pricing, in-kind transfers, or cash transfers) should be an integral part of this cost recovery policy.

Intergovernmental grants and revenue redistribution

Whatever design is eventually adopted, some imbalance between revenue and expenditure within certain fiscal units is unavoidable. The Federation of Bosnia and Herzegovina may therefore need to consider developing some type of intergovernmental grants or revenue-sharing system. It is important to keep in mind that the political strains induced by such a transfer system were a key factor leading to the collapse of the former Yugoslavia. In designing a transfer system, therefore, great care must be taken to minimize potential sources of political tension. A system of grants is generally used to exploit economies of scale in collecting certain taxes, provide some degree of equity in resource allocation, and overcome certain externalities in the delivery of certain services, such as vaccinations against communicable diseases or universal primary education (local governments are likely to underprovide such services in the absence of a grants system that encourages the local government to expand service provision until its social marginal cost is equal to its social marginal benefit). In Bosnia and Herzegovina (as in almost all formerly socialist economies) revenues are usually transferred on the basis of where revenues are collected (the so-called "derivation principle"). This is one way of pursuing a subset of the above-mentioned objectives. Alternative sharing or grant schemes will be needed, however, if redistribution across cantons or municipalities is considered desirable and politically feasible. This approach could redistribute the proceeds from either a single tax or a pool of tax revenues. The most important thing is that the formula applied to distribute funds across municipalities be based on objective and transparent indicators. A system of grants based on negotiated formulas or ad hoc procedures would be particularly inappropriate for Bosnia and Herzegovina, given the lingering distrust still prevailing among different groups in society.

Looking beyond the transition period, the Federation of Bosnia and Herzegovina will need to agree on a preferred combination of grant financing and own-source tax financing for its cantons and municipalities. This preferred combination should take into account the advantages and disadvantages of each financing source. Own-source tax financing is often preferred to grant financing because it allows for a greater local discretion in setting rates in line with local demand for services and enhanced accountability in the use of locally raised funds. The key disadvantages of own-source tax financing are that it may lead to a more inequitable distribution of public goods, since some municipalities are richer than others; it may entail diseconomies of scale in the administration of certain taxes; and it could lead to wider disparities in tax rates and tax competition among cantons or municipalities.

Commission on Intergovernmental Fiscal Relations

Three significant problems exist or can be expected from the establishment of a Federation system. First, fiscal imbalances will arise whatever the system chosen, and these need to be corrected. Second, there is inadequate information on which to base decisions about proper tax base sharing, tax assignment, and intergovernmental transfers. Third, there are significant variations in budgeting procedures in the Federation. The International Monetary Fund has recommended that a Commission on Fiscal Intergovernmental Relations be established to address these problems. The commission should be staffed with fiscal experts from the various regions so that it will be viewed as a professional and impartial body.

The commission should focus on four interrelated functions:

• Design policies that minimize needs and resource imbalances. Variations in service delivery and revenue burdens must be regularly evaluated, requiring the collection of economic, demographic, and fiscal information that is comparable across municipalities and cantons. Collection of such data is also important to build confidence in the system and to ensure that such imbalances are dealt with transparently. The commission should create a high-quality database and a system through which the budgets and financial reports of all subnational governments are reported in a consistent manner.

• Assist or arbitrate in the establishment of cities and cantons. Although the commission would not have any authority over intergovernmental cooperative agreements among municipalities, it would offer technical assistance, establish norms for these agreements, and help resolve disputes that may arise.

• Provide general technical assistance at the municipal and cantonal level in budgeting.

• Coordinate all research on issues relating to fiscal federalism, its evolution, and the future fiscal stability of the Federation.

Fiscal Structure for the Serb Republic

In one respect, the issues in reforming the Serb Republic's fiscal structure are different from those of the Federation because it is expected that the Republic's unitary structure will continue. In another respect, however, the Serb Republic faces challenges similar to those that are facing the Federation. These include establishment of a system of user charges for public goods and services; establishment of effective customs administration and coordination with the Federation on policies and procedures; rationalization of the fiscal relation between the republican government and municipalities; and reform of pension systems and health care financing (see section IV). More review will be needed before concrete proposals can be made concerning the reform of fiscal structures in the Serb Republic.

IV. TOWARD SETTING UP A MARKET ECONOMY

Setting up a market economy in Bosnia and Herzegovina will require major adjustments in two broad areas. The first area involves *redefining the role of the State*, moving away from the all-encompassing government functions performed in the past and toward a more focused facilitation and regulatory role. In a modern market economy, the State has four key responsibilities: maintaining a sound macroeconomic framework, establishing and enforcing an appropriate legal and regulatory framework, providing or regulating the provision of basic public goods and services, and establishing safety net mechanisms for the most disadvantaged members of society. The second area involves *transforming the enterprise and banking system* so that it can compete efficiently in a market environment. Due to the particular circumstances facing Bosnia and Herzegovina, this transformation should follow three principles: removing old stocks of debts and liabilities in banks and enterprises from current operations and addressing them separately to allow the cleanup of balance sheets, the privatization of banks and firms, and the reactivation of operations in viable enterprises to take place as quickly as possible; minimizing the fiscal cost of resolving outstanding liabilities; and following a regional approach to the privatization of enterprises in order to avoid political complications and other implementation constraints. There are important linkages between redefining the role of the State and transforming the bank and enterprise sectors. For example, private investment in the restructured banks offered for privatization will not proceed unless the legal framework within which the privatized banks will subsequently operate remains undefined. Both efforts must take place concurrently for maximum effectiveness.

New Role for the Government

Bosnia and Herzegovina has been remarkably successful in maintaining orderly macroeconomic conditions since mid-1994. Experience in other countries has shown that this is an important but insufficient step for restoring economic growth. Additional measures are needed to create an incentive structure that is conducive to faster growth. In this regard, the experience in other countries points to the importance of the private sector and the advantages of maintaining open, market-friendly policies. It is telling that no country in Central and Eastern Europe has been able to achieve stable growth through a return to State-led, centrally managed development policies.

It is tempting to argue that special conditions in Bosnia and Herzegovina—a fragile peace, large numbers of refugees, devastated infrastructure, weak private institutions, and collapsed markets—require direct government involvement in the recovery of domestic production. But this argument is not supported by postconflict experiences elsewhere. In fact, recovery in Europe and Japan after World War II and more recently in Lebanon have been spearheaded by the private sector. At any rate, Bosnia and Herzegovina's extreme fiscal constraints leave no alternative than to let the private sector take the lead in managing the economic recovery. The resources for any large-scale government investment simply do not exist. And if more resources were to become available, say from donors, it would be extremely risky to channel them in that direction.

The focus on the private sector as the engine of growth does not mean that the public sector is henceforth unimportant. Quite the contrary—how the government functions and what policies it implements are crucially important in preparing the field for a private sector-led recovery. The transition to a market economy, however, requires that the government divest itself of old responsibilities and focus on the four responsibilities described earlier: macroeconomic stability, legal and regulatory frameworks, public goods, and social safety nets such as pension and health The government's role in maintaining macroeconomic stability was already discussed in section III. This section focuses on the remaining areas.

Establishing a Medium-Term Legal and Regulatory Framework

Setting up a comprehensive legal and regulatory framework in Bosnia and Herzegovina is of primary importance for the medium-term development of a private sector-based market economy. Private investment capital, both domestic and foreign, will require a secure legal and regulatory framework to reduce the risks of doing business. In some cases additional legislation is needed to enhance the effectiveness of existing laws; in others completely new laws need to be designed. Key areas in need of further development and clarification include:

- *Property laws,* to set clear rules of ownership and control.

- *Contract laws* and related procedures for dispute resolution (in-court, out-of-court), to establish a legal framework for commercial bargaining and to ensure the fair enforcement of private contracts. This area is closely related to the clarification of property laws and the use of collateral for secured transactions.

- *Company* and *foreign investment laws,* to provide for easy entry of new enterprises into the market, including a *bankruptcy law* to enforce contracts and establish a mechanism for exit.

- *Regulatory policies,* to address market failures, whether by inhibiting the distortions of unregulated monopolies, forcing firms to disclose information needed by the market, or providing incentives for enterprises to internalize external environmental costs.

- *Labor law,* to set basic ground rules for employment and industrial relations, including the facilitation of labor shedding by enterprises, supported by social assistance if needed. Restrictions and barriers to labor mobility, such as complicated labor shedding procedures, expensive severance payments, and requirements relating to long notification periods and to finding alternative employment—as required by the current legal system inherited from the former Yugoslavia—should be removed to facilitate the restructuring of enterprises and banks.

- *Accounting* and *auditing laws* and standards based on international rules, to provide the basis for compilation and disclosure of uniform and meaningful financial information.

With special regard to the legal, regulatory, and supervisory framework in the financial sector, several draft laws are being prepared in both Entities as well as at the State level to define the roles of the central bank, bank supervision, commercial banks, and insurance and capital markets. In addition to the enactment of these laws, prudential banking regulations are needed for effective licensing and supervision. This includes regulations that are clear and provide practical guidelines for implementation and enforcement of the law concerning licensing standards, such as minimum capital requirements, scope of operations, shareholder and management requirements, and reporting requirements; capital adequacy standards that properly reflect risk management safeguards; loan classification systems that reflect proper risk weights and adequately account for delinquencies and interest capitalization; loan concentration to large borrowers and insider borrowers; foreign exchange operations and exposure to contain systemic risk; and credit policy and procedures to enhance the prospects for successful credit management. These efforts will have to include new accounting standards in line with accepted international practices.

Direct Government Provision versus Regulation of Public Goods

The war has caused many public services to collapse. As Bosnia and Herzegovina begins the task of restoring the capacity to provide these services, it faces the choice of either having the public sector provide these services directly or of having the private sector provide these services under an appropriate regulatory and supervisory framework developed by the government. Although the *private sector* will bear the main burden of reconstructing the country, the private sector, left on its own, tends to not provide sufficient amounts of public goods and services. In some cases, this is because private providers do not capture all the costs imposed or benefits derived from the consumption of a public goods. In other cases, the production of the good in question involves a natural monopoly, providing the private producer with an incentive to charge monopoly prices and, thus, usually to deliver a less than sufficient amount and quality of services.

While the traditional way of dealing with this problem used to be to have the public sector own and operate the production facilities and, thus directly provide the public good, over the past decade there has been a worldwide tendency to opt for the alternative—*regulation of the provision of public services by the private sector.* For many countries this has been the favored solution in many utility and infrastructure sectors, including electricity generation and distribution, telecommunications, ports, and urban transport. In other sectors, such as primary health and education services, a combination of direct provision and regulated private provision has generally been adopted. While there are no fixed rules governing the provision of public goods for all cases, there is mounting evidence worldwide that the private sector can effectively deliver public goods and services provided that an appropriate regulatory framework is established and enforced.

Rebuilding Social Safety Nets

With the collapse of production capacity, employment and incomes in Bosnia and Herzegovina plummeted in direct proportion to the fall of GDP. Whereas in 1990 nearly 1 million people were employed in the country's territory, fewer than 250,000 are currently registered as employed in both Entities. Furthermore, earnings are largely symbolic for most of those now employed. This is especially true of the Bosniac areas of the Federation and in the Serb Republic, where monthly wages are estimated to have averaged about DM 30 in 1995. Although average monthly earnings in 1995 were higher in the Croat majority areas of the Federation (DM 350), they are still low by historical standards. Cash transfers through the pension system, child allowances, and other entitlement programs have also declined in line with the drop in earnings.

In the wake of these developments, the incomes of most households are no longer adequate to provide for minimum subsistence needs. About 80 percent of the population in the Federation depends on emergency food aid for its survival. In November 1995, such aid was provided to 90 percent of the Bosniac population and 30 percent of the Croat population. The per capita value of in-kind emergency assistance has averaged about $170 (DM 252) a year since 1992.

Economic recovery is expected to advance quickly in Bosnia and Herzegovina following the implementation of the Peace Agreement. Recovery should generate immediate income opportunities for many people who currently rely on humanitarian assistance for their survival. For many others, however, it may take longer or they may be bypassed altogether. These groups will require a well-targeted cash transfer system. Such a system will also be required with the phasing out of emergency food aid programs. An Emergency Social Fund for cash transfers to meet the essential consumption needs of the poorest households has been established under an Emergency Recovery Credit approved by the World Bank in February 1996, with co-funding from other donors. Payments through this fund, based on declarations of household incomes, will provide temporary cash relief over a period of one year, permitting the revival of better-targeted social assistance programs similar to those that existed before the war, involving income proxies (such as, employment status and age) and documentary evidence on household incomes. The longer-term subsistence needs of the poor are expected to be addressed through the restoration of benefit programs for particular vulnerable groups, such as pensions for the elderly and disabled, unemployment insurance for people experiencing a temporary job loss, and health insurance.

Pension Finance Reform. The pension system requires special attention. During the war the pension system was split into three pension plans: one in the Serb Republic and two in the Federation. All three pension plans inherited the former Yugoslavia's pension system which, like almost every system in the formerly socialist economies, was financially unsustainable, managerially deficient, and poor at delivering services. All three pension systems are under an exceptional degree of financial stress. Pensions have plummeted since 1991, forcing many pensioners into conditions of extreme poverty. Solving these problems will not be easy. The first requirement is to establish measures that stabilize the situation in the short run. Short-run stability will facilitate the development and implementation of prudent and sustainable policies that promote economic growth and provide a floor of protection to workers and their families who have lost earnings due to age, death, or disability.

In the plan started in the Croat majority areas, pensions are paid at a flat rate of DM 55 (raised to an average of DM 65 through special supplements). A flat rate is used because during the war the earnings-record information stored in Sarajevo could not be accessed to calculate earnings-related pensions. In the rest of the Federation, most pensions are paid at an average rate of about DM 13, with some variation in individual pensions related to prepension work histories and earnings. These pensions have plummeted as wages have fallen to levels that are unacceptably low. Pensions in the Serb Republic have also been paid at a very minimal level, although the Serb authorities have claimed that there have been no arrears in pension payments.

Both Federation systems are in arrears. In the one started in the Croat majority areas, no pensions at all were paid in 1992 or 1993. Pensions in the Bosniac part of the Federation were paid erratically, with payments currently six months behind schedule throughout most of the system.

All systems collect payroll taxes for pensions. The system started in the Croat majority area continues to operate primarily as an autonomous pension fund, while the fund that functions in the Bosniac majority areas has been completely integrated with the government budget, as has been the system in the Serb Republic. With low employment and earnings, contribution rates have become extraordinarily high. In the system of the Croat majority, area pension contributions alone account for 17.5 percent of gross wages. In the Bosniac system, contributions were recently reduced to 24 percent, including employee and employer portions. It is likely that the contribution rate for pensions in the Serb Republic are also very high.

All systems have suffered from a severe decline in the number of contributors relative to pensioners. The low ratio of contributors to pensioners, at virtually one-to-one, is particularly striking in a region that used to be characterized by a relatively young population. While Bosnia and Herzegovina is unlikely to face an age structure as unfavorable as other Central and Eastern European countries (such as Bulgaria), with population losses and declining birth rates the structure may be shifting to one that is less favorable in terms of its potential to provide future support for an older population.

At the present time, pension fund administration and planning is untenable due to postwar uncertainties and the lack of timely information on which normal pension systems rely. For example, data on unemployment, wages, and even population are unreliable or unavailable. The number of returning pensioners and the number of returning workers cannot be accurately estimated. Even information on the number of contributors is uncertain.

Under the old system, replacement rates were extremely high, leaving no room for the development of investment-based pensions. Normal retirement was set at early ages for both sexes, with many opportunities for even earlier retirement. Data indicate that an unusually large proportion of the pensioner population was receiving disability pensions in 1991. Moreover, the system was never self-financing. Thus systemic changes would have been required in the country's pension systems, even if the war had not taken place. As evidence, pension systems in Croatia and the former Yugoslav Republic of Macedonia are undergoing substantial policy changes because the inherited system has proved unaffordable.

Basic pension reform is clearly needed, given fundamental weaknesses in the current arrangements and the unaffordable legislative provisions inherited from the former Yugoslavia. Pension reform leading to an entirely new pension system will need to proceed rapidly, but carefully, given the economic devastation and the need to build new institutions throughout the Federation and the State. Consequently, a multistage process can be envisaged that replaces both the old law and the current situation with a three-tier pension scheme. The *first tier* would help ensure a minimum floor of protection for all pensioners. An Entity-level *minimum, flat-rate pension* should be developed that would initially be funded by a *fixed contribution* per employee and supplemented by donor funding. In subsequent years the flat-rate contribution could be instituted through payroll tax contributions that would be raised in 1997 and 1998 as the donor supplement is phased out. In the longer term, the payroll tax for pension contributions would be limited to a maximum of 15 percent of gross wages.

Once these initial measures are taken, a second tier of earnings-related pensions could be instituted, probably to be provided at the cantonal or intercantonal level. If this second tier is related to earnings and years of service, issues such as the age of entitlement, the benefits formula, other eligibility criteria, and postentitlement indexing should be addressed. Since these reforms are contingent on anticipated changes in other key sectors, including labor law reform, the timetable for pension reform must be closely coordinated with related measures.

While the old system has built up a substantial backlog of arrears due to the nonpayment or late payment of pensions, *the arrears issue should not be addressed within the rubric of pension reform.* Instead, the new pension system should be designed to start with a clean slate. Pension arrears could be discussed within the framework of the settlement of all other unpaid claims on government discussed earlier. Once the new pension system is instituted, no further claims for payment based on the eligibility criteria and benefits formula of past legislation would be allowed.

Finally, a third, voluntary tier of investment-based pensions would be instituted in several years. This tier would be expected to develop slowly with appropriate prudential guidelines for investments and other regulatory standards. Plans could be employment-based, occupational, or individual. Design and implementation of the third-tier system would provide complete pension reform.

Health reform. Like the pension system, the health financing system has major fiscal implications, as well as implications for the size of the State. Bosnia and Herzegovina's previous health system was also split into three systems as a result of the war. In recent years, health care within the Federation area has been financed from two sources. In the Croat majority areas, an insurance fund paid for health care, primarily by financing the salaries of health sector staff. In the Bosniac majority area, a former health insurance fund was incorporated into the government budget. Similarly, health care in Serb Republic was also consolidated into the budget. In all areas payroll taxes (at 12.5 percent of gross wages) were the intended source of funds. Because of the shortage of funds, physical supplies and consumable goods have been donated by external sources. Recurrent spending, when it has occurred, has been largely limited to salary payments.

The health care sector faces the triple challenge of creating a new governance structure, rehabilitating or reconstructing the sector's physical infrastructure, and resuming fundamental sectoral reforms required by the transition to a market-oriented economy. Three immediate priorities are to maintain the effectiveness of the basic health care delivery system despite severe financial constraints; to establish priorities for a program of effective capital investment; and to develop a plan for medium-term reform of the sector and its financing. Six issues in health care financing stand out: the resolution of past arrears in payments for wages and salaries as well as for suppliers, immediate sources of financing, future financing arrangements, the collection of contributions to health financing schemes, new payment mechanisms, and the coordinating efforts to normalize health care financing with plans by nongovernmental organizations and other donors to phase out emergency relief. More study will be needed before concrete proposals can be made for fundamental health sector reform.

Enterprise and Banking Reform

Enterprises and banks in Bosnia and Herzegovina inherited most of their institutional and structural characteristics from the Yugoslav system of market socialism and self-management. Enterprises were socially-owned, endowed with assets owned by society at large (there was no State property) and formally run by workers councils. In principle, key enterprise decisions were made by workers. In practice, however, decision making was in the hands of management formally selected by workers councils and tacitly approved by the political system. The system was decentralized and allowed competition in the product market but restricted competition and mobility in the labor and financial markets. Commercial banks were the only source of institutional capital, and bank credit was the only form of financing for enterprises. Banks were owned by enterprises and controlled by large enterprises, both as owners and debtors, who used them to obtain financing on favorable terms. In addition, banks were often pressed by the government to finance priority projects.

Current Enterprise Structure and Performance

Since 1992, parallel legal frameworks have been developed in the Bosniac-, Croat-, and Serb majority areas of Bosnia and Herzegovina. In each area, pragmatic steps were taken to improve corporate governance, prevent asset stripping and pave the way for private investment. In the Bosniac majority area and Serb majority area, line ministries appointed new company management boards under temporary laws, and special laws were approved by each area's Parliament to convert all socially-owned enterprises to State ownership. In the Croat majority area, the authorities also appointed company boards for each locality based on proposals from local communities. Progress toward private ownership of enterprises occurred much more quickly in this area, with about two-thirds of employment and nearly 60 percent of the current book value of enterprises in private hands or under public-private ownership.

In the Croat majority area, more numerous private enterprises, coupled with a liberal foreign investment policy and better links abroad than the rest of the country, have contributed to increased capacity utilization. Production has already recovered to 85 percent of the prewar level. Production in the Bosniac majority area was restarted in a number of enterprises at the end of 1994, notably in food processing, textiles and apparel, leather and shoes, and soap and hygienic products. The majority of prewar conglomerates have been separated into their constituent parts, most of which are idle. By contrast, private enterprises and some smaller, socially-owned enterprises have become quite active, especially in commerce and transport services. Still, overall production remains depressed at just 5-10 percent of its prewar level. Similarly, the economic embargo against the Serb Republic seriously undermined the performance of its enterprise sector, and only with the recent lifting of the embargo have the prospects for increased production in this area improved.

Current Bank Structure and Performance

As with the other sectors, the war broke the banking sector into three systems. Parallel banking systems and regulatory frameworks have developed. There are currently forty-nine banks operating in Bosnia and Herzegovina, of which twenty-eight report to the Sarajevo-based National Bank of Bosnia and Herzegovina (NBBH), eight report to the Mostar-based authorities, and thirteen report to the Ministry of Finance and central bank in the Serb Republic in Banja Luka. Nearly half of these banks are private (including all those in the Federation area), while the other banks are descendants of several old banks owned by large, socially owned enterprises. On a book value basis, these large banks account for most of the assets on the balance sheet of the aggregated banking sector. While the private banks are not burdened by the problems inherited by the public banks, their capital base is small (total of DM 5 million, likely to average DM 300,000 after loan losses are included). These banks provide mostly short-term credits to finance commercial activities and carry interest rates of 2-6 percent a month. Confidence in the banks is very limited, both because of the war and because of the freezing of foreign currency deposits at the start of the war, so that few persons place their savings in banks.

Between 90 and 95 percent of the banking sector's assets are nonperforming and, for practical reasons, should be written off. (The banks in the Croat majority area may already have written off much of their prewar foreign exchange-denominated exposure, or their foreign [Croatian] shareholders have assumed these liabilities.) Without accounting for needed writeoffs and adjustments, the banking sector's balance sheet, as reported to the NBBH, consists of three major components: households' foreign currency deposits in the banks (on the liabilities side) and corresponding claims on the former National Bank of Yugoslavia in Belgrade (on the assets side); foreign borrowing from international financial institutions, commercial banks, and foreign governments (on the liabilities side), which banks extended in foreign currency credits to domestic State enterprises (on the assets side); and other assets and liabilities denominated in local currency. Households' foreign exchange deposits have been frozen for several years, and the corresponding claims in Belgrade are assumed to be worthless. The loans extended to enterprises are nonperforming because the projects they financed have been discontinued, with many of their assets having been physically damaged or destroyed by the war or by neglect. The value of assets and liabilities denominated in domestic currency has shrunk to insignificance due to the 1992-93 hyperinflation and collapse of economic activity.

Transforming the Enterprise and Banking Sectors

While the authorities have made progress in implementing various important enterprise and banking reforms, much more is needed to fundamentally transform the economy into a sound, largely private, market economy. In the financial sector, a key problem is the burden of inherited bad loans and foreign exchange deposit liabilities. In the enterprise sector, social ownership and self-management continue to create inappropriate incentives for investment and production decisions. The prewar web between enterprises and banks—characterized by enterprise ownership of major banks and bank lending to major corporate owners—would, if left unreformed, cause a major misallocation of resources as economic activity recovers. A comprehensive reform package needs to be prepared that takes into account the links between the war and impaired enterprises, bad loans and frozen deposits in the banking sector, and the problems of overstaffing and need for labor redeployment.

The central objective of structural reforms in this sector is to create a diversified economy in which privately owned enterprises make independent decisions on production and marketing and private banks provide intermediation services to support the investment requirements of these enterprises. Within such a framework, large and State-owned industrial and commercial conglomerates, as well as the large banks, are likely to be replaced by a much greater number of small and medium-sized banks and enterprises. To some extent this trend has already started. To achieve the ultimate objective of creating a private market economy in the medium term, this trend should be encouraged further with the privatization of banks and enterprises. At the same time, the legal and regulatory framework needs to be developed to ensure effective market competition and to prevent major bank failures that could have adverse systemic consequences. The main role of the government during this transition period is to manage the privatization process and undertake the institutional reforms needed to implement the new legal and regulatory framework.

Given these circumstances, three fundamental principles should guide the reform of the enterprise and banking sector in Bosnia and Herzegovina. First, the sector's stock liabilities need to be separated from current operations so that they do not inhibit economic recovery. Second, the fiscal costs of settling the outstanding liabilities of the banking sector need to be minimized. Third, privatization should take into account the ethnic diversity of the country, especially since most enterprises and banks are controlled by distinct ethnic groups. Thus privatization may be most effective if it is organized in a regionally decentralized manner.

Strategy for Privatization

A regionally based approach to privatization would allow programs to be implemented regionally (at the Republic level in one Entity and at the cantonal or municipal levels in the Federation) through regional privatization agencies, while most disputes would be settled at the State or Federation/Serb Republic level. Items in dispute include bank claims on enterprises, enterprise claims (arrears) on one another, frozen foreign exchange deposit claims on banks, and claims on the government for wage and pension arrears, restitution, or war-related claims. Most of these items would be transferred out of the current institutions to a settlement mechanism established at the Federation/Serb Republic or State level, while some (such as bad bank loans and corresponding liabilities denominated in foreign currency and linked to prospective Paris and London Club negotiations) would be placed with the State

Ministry of Finance. Under this approach, enterprise debts would be drastically reduced and bank liabilities would be removed from the balance sheet, leaving enterprises financially restructured and ready for quick privatization. Faster privatization could take place in regions/cantons that are ready, without forcing them to wait or accommodate other region/cantons' preferences, as would be the case under a more centralized privatization approach.

The recommended regional approach to privatizing enterprises and smaller, socially owned banks in Bosnia and Herzegovina comprises the following key steps:

- Transform banks and enterprises from social ownership to public ownership.

- After the State/public sector (governments at the Entity level in most cases) assumes control, appoint new management teams that are not responsible for those enterprises that formerly controlled the banks.

- Carve out all bad assets and corresponding liabilities and equity. Most likely, all pre-1991 assets should be carved out, as well as some post-1991 ones. Following a short work-out period, this would leave the banks financially restructured and ready to be privatized.

- Separate the carved-out assets from the banks and place the bad loans and corresponding liabilities with the government authorities and the frozen foreign exchange deposits into a settlement mechanism to be set up by the government and dealt with separately.

- Set up a Regional Privatization Agency (RPA's) in districts and cantons for the Federation and perhaps one agency in the Serb Republic. All assets (banks and enterprises) to be privatized would be governed by one of these regional privatization agencies as the representative of the Entity government as owner. Also, it will be necessary to set up a State privatization agency and to establish consistent operating guidelines for the regional agencies and to settle interjurisdictional disputes. A "sunset provision" specifying the duration of the regional agencies could help accelerate the privatization process. Privatization of the large banks would have to be implemented by the Entity level privatization agency, or even the State privatization agency.

- Initiate the privatization process through a combination of privatization mechanisms, including public auctions, tenders, and share offerings. Privatization certificates or passbooks would be offered as noncash compensation for claims on the government (for example, frozen foreign exchange accounts, wage arrears, restitution claims).

The authorities managing the privatization process need to establish from the outset a list of public enterprises that are *not to* be privatized, with the understanding that all enterprises that are not on this list will be privatized. (In the banking sector it is assumed that all publicly-owned banks will be either privatized or liquidated.) Also, in carving out enterprise assets (such as equity in banks and frozen bank deposits) and liabilities (borrowings owed to banks), it will be important to separate out assets that have no connection with the core business conducted by the enterprise. This should include, for example, apartments owned by large enterprises and leased to their employees (there are about 190,000 enterprise-owned apartments in the Federation alone).

Settlement of Past Claims and Arrears

A particular problem is the large number of claims on the government, including the claims of individuals (unpaid wages and pensions, restitution for postwar nationalization, claims on frozen foreign currency accounts, claims for damage and other losses arising from the war) and claims between and among the government and socially owned institutions (bad bank loans, enterprise-government arrears, and interenterprise arrears). Settling all these claims from available fiscal resources is well beyond the government's fiscal capacity. Therefore *no major fiscal resources should be provided for the settlement of claims*. A substantial portion of the claims of individuals could be settled by exchanging them for privatization certificates that can be used along with cash for privatization transactions.

Settlement through the provision of privatization certificates could be envisaged for three types of claims: (i) claims on bank deposits in foreign exchange that were frozen in 1991; (ii) restitution claims, where these cannot or should not be settled in kind with the property being claimed; and (iii) claims resulting from wage and pension arrears and by veterans based on their length of service and the degree of injury or other personal loss they may have suffered.

These privatization certificates could later be used, together with cash, to purchase publicly owned assets that could be offered for sale in the near future, including housing, agricultural and forest land, enterprises and commercial banks.

As the next step, the government needs to develop criteria for *prioritizing claims* in the settlement mechanism (through the weights assigned to each claim as the claims are translated into privatization certificates). In determining the priority of claims, social equity considerations will have to be balanced against economic efficiency considerations. While many of the elements of this settlement mechanism would be captured in specific legislation on restitution, housing, and privatization, umbrella legislation on the settlement concept is needed to define the claims to be incorporated in the settlement mechanism and to describe how these claims will be exchanged for assets. Preparation in this regard is more advanced in the

Federation part of Bosnia and Herzegovina. The Federation government intends to submit such a global Settlement Law to Parliament by the end of April 1996. No plan has yet been worked out in this regard in the Serb Republic.

Particular consideration should be given to providing some measure of recognition for frozen foreign exchange accounts that were mandatorily placed in the National Bank of Yugoslavia (headquartered in Belgrade) prior to independence. The total value of these deposits is estimated to be DM 1.65 billion. About 80 percent of all households had accounts with less than DM 1000. To provide compensation for the loss of these deposits, the State government, or the Federation government and the Serb Republic government in coordination with the State government, could consider issuing certificates—that can be used in various ways (see paragraph 146)--up to a maximum amount per citizen, based on existing documentation. Regarding claims on the National Bank of Yugoslavia for lost foreign exchange deposits, it should be clear that the banks cannot deal adequately with this issue. Such claims, together with other claims on the Federal Republic of Yugoslavia, are an issue between sovereign states and thus are best confined to agents of the State.

Other claims on the State include restitution claims for expropriated properties, wage and pension arrears, including those to the military and other personnel. These claims still need to be quantified. Concerning claims between banks and enterprises, net bank claims on enterprises should be applied against enterprise ownership in banks. This approach would lead to a massive writeoff of enterprises' equity shares in the socially owned banks, with the result that the government would effectively renationalize the banks, facilitating their subsequent privatization.

Public housing is potentially important asset in the settlement mechanism. Information is gathered at the present only on situation in the Federation. Although more than 80 percent of all housing in the Federation of Bosnia and Herzegovina is already in private hands, a significant number of housing units is owned by public enterprises and the State or municipal governments. The Federation government intends to privatize these units, in most cases giving current tenants the right of first refusal to buy flats that they legally occupy. A Housing Privatization Law is needed in the Federation to carry out such a transaction in addition to an overall Privatization Law to provide a framework for the privatization process. A proper legal framework for housing and apartments is also needed to recognize ownership rights with great transparency, avoid straining public sector (in this case municipal) budgets with maintenance and repair costs, and be consistent with needs for shelter during the postwar period. At a minimum, housing legislation should segregate public housing from public enterprise ownership to facilitate the privatization of enterprises. To begin the process of privatizing housing, an inventory of housing units needs to be made, together with a status report on the current ownership and occupancy of each unit to sort out tenancy rights. For purposes of speed and simplicity, regional privatization agencies could coordinate the housing privatization process at the local level.

The approach described here conforms with the preferences expressed by the Federation authorities. An expert privatization team was appointed in the Federation in mid-1995 to review privatization issues and options and to prepare initial drafts of necessary supporting legislation. A draft Settlement Law, draft Restitution Law, draft Housing Privatization Law, a draft Privatization Law, and draft Privatization Agency Laws have been prepared. In the Serb Republic, the authorities are contemplating revising the former Yugoslavia's laws on privatization in order to accelerate the process. Preparation for privatization is at the beginning stage.

Issues in Banking and Financial Sector Reforms

A quick recovery in output will inevitably require a functioning banking system. Firms will need working capital and at some point investment will recover. Moreover, across Eastern Europe, banks have played crucial roles in the privatization process and, to varying degrees, in enterprise restructuring. Finally, banks still play a major role in mobilizing private savings in most economies. Thus jump-starting the banking system should be at the top of the policy agenda. Previously, banks basically provided blank checks to enterprises—who often owned the banks to begin with—and rediscounted the loans at the central banks, thus fatally undermining stabilization policy. The banking system will need to be reconstructed, but if financial stability is to be achieved, the flaws of the former Yugoslavia's banking system should be carefully avoided. These problems fall into two general areas: issues of financial system design and transition arrangements.

Financial system design. Banking reform requires action in four areas. *First*, banks need to operate in a clear legal environment. This requires, at a minimum, laws on commercial banking and on the role of the central bank. Given commercial banks' poor record on bank supervision and corporate governance, banking laws will have to be very specific on corporate governance structures.

Second, a legal structure is meaningless unless there is a supervision machinery to make sure the laws are adhered to. Current plans lean toward a banking commission model of bank supervision and enforcement. The supervision role may eventually be transferred to the central bank once that institution's mandate is expanded. There are, however, good reasons to maintain the banking commission model for the enforcement part and possibly for supervision. Bank supervisors have an incentive to delay intervention since the need to intervene can often be interpreted as a signal of lax supervision in earlier periods. This is the main argument for separating supervision from acting on signals of distress. Whatever model is chosen, the corresponding laws authorizing the supervision agency need to be very specific on when and how the agency will intervene when standards of good behavior are violated.

Of course, supervision can only function with adequate information provision. Information provision depends critically on accounting standards, the *third* issue. To the extent that generally accepted accounting standards are not adhered to, technical assistance to this end should be a priority. This is of particular importance in the area of loan classification and treatment of capitalized interest. Adequate loan classification is key for a correct calculation of capital value and is essential if capital adequacy ratios similar to those developed by the Bank for International Settlements (BIS) are to be used in a meaningful way in the regulatory setup.

Fourth, banks have to develop a proper corporate structure. Particular care should be taken to remove corporate owners from positions of control. Insider lending is developing as the major cause of banking distress in many countries and insider lending is extremely difficult to control if major borrowers in fact control the bank. The widely prevailing problem of bank insolvency actually points the way toward the necessary ownership reform. Existing corporate-held equity can simply be wiped out by imposing proper loan classification procedures and capital adequacy rules. This will in many cases show that existing equity has been wiped out already, allowing a takeover by the government. This procedure should be a prerequisite for a proper privatization strategy. The relatively large number of banks in Bosnia and Herzegovina (about three times as many as, say, Mexico, a country with a GDP more than a hundred times bigger than Bosnia's) suggests that a process of consolidation and tightening up of licensing procedures may also be called for.

Two general issues also require attention. *First*, several points mentioned above raise issues concerning the type of banking sector. Bosnia and Herzegovina is likely to opt eventually for universal banking, if only because such a structure will facilitate eventual integration with Western Europe.[3] However, unless carefully organized, such developments may result in major regulatory difficulties. In a fragile banking environment, transparency is crucial for sound banking to emerge. This argues strongly against allowing, for example, the type of banking-insurance conglomerates that are now being formed across Western Europe and that, in a very different form, also exist in the former Soviet Union. The banking law

---

[3] Unless carefully prepared, however, such a structure may create major regulatory difficulties. In a fragile banking environment transparency is crucial for sound banking to emerge. This argues strongly against allowing bank-insurance companies and other conglomerates that are now being formed across Western Europe and that, in a different form, also exist in the states of the former Soviet Union. Legislation and regulations need to ensure that systemic risk is minimized. From that viewpoint, such conglomerations should be explicitly ruled out or forced to be formed as fully separate subsidiaries. Similarly, West European-style corporate governance mechanisms involve equity holdings or the exercise of proxy voting rights. In this case also, transparency and the need to avoid soft budget constraints in banks with regards to their corporate clients require that special attention be paid to maintaining separate institutional identities of banks and enterprises.

could explicitly rule out insurance activities or require them to be undertaken in a fully separate subsidiary.[4]

Similarly, equity holdings or exercise of proxy voting rights may be necessary in establishing effective enterprise restructuring and Western Europe-style corporate governance mechanisms. Again, however, transparency and the need to avoid soft budget constraints in the bank with respect to its corporate clients require at least confinement of such activities to a separate subsidiary.

Second, establishing some sort of deposit insurance may be necessary to convince the population to once again entrust their savings to the banking system. But care should be taken not to introduce deposit insurance in the current lax regulatory structure without careful caps on potential exposure. First of all, deposit insurance should be limited to household deposits. If corporate deposits are covered, too, then no one has any incentive to monitor management. And in any case the social argument for deposit protection does not hold for corporate deposits. Second, since large depositors may also be able and willing to monitor management, some countries also put a cap on the size of private deposits or on the amount insured. In practice such limitations are rarely enforced, however.

A final point on deposit insurance is that its introduction makes the task of building effective regulatory institutions all the more urgent. Deposit insurance encourages undue risk taking by managers because their downside risk exposure is covered; to avoid excessive taxpayer expense, careful management supervision in this respect is of the utmost importance. A strategy that has been followed in several Central and Eastern European countries is to introduce deposit insurance but to limit it to household deposits, with a fairly low cap on the amount insured (say, $1,500) and linked to banks that meet capital adequacy requirements that comply with BIS rules.

Transition Issues. Even if all the financial design issues covered so far could be resolved, Bosnia's banks are not sufficiently developed to fulfill the duties of a modern banking sector. The banking system has effectively been reduced to an agent for the execution of payments within an unsatisfactory mechanism. The banking system's intermediary role and its role in corporate governance have basically come to a standstill. Banks not only suffer from the traditional Eastern European problem of loan portfolio deterioration due to enterprise loan servicing problems, but also carry a considerable burden as a consequence of the disorderly breakup of the former Yugoslavia. In particular, the banks have considerable foreign exchange deposits on their liabilities side matched by unrecoverable foreign exchange claims on the central bank of the former Yugoslavia in Belgrade.

---

[4] A bank could still act as an agent for an insurance company and sell policies through its branch network, but it is essential that the bank itself does not underwrite any risk.

Claims on Yugoslavia and old foreign exchange deposits There should be no doubt that the banks themselves cannot adequately deal with the problems of the former Yugoslavia's banking system. As mentioned above, claims on Yugoslavia are now an issue between sovereign states and are thus best confined to agents of the State. Slovenia transferred most such claims to its central bank in order to remove this issue from commercial banks' balance sheets. These claims can be incorporated into any general debt settlement for the republics of the former Yugoslavia if there ever is such a settlement or, possibly more realistically, simply be written off.

The Bad Loan Problem. Strategies to deal with bad loan problems are often designed in such a way that collection incentives are preserved for the bank without allowing them to become victims of the liquidation bias embedded in most bankruptcy practices. The objective, then, is to rescue as many enterprises as possible as going concerns. However, the situation in Bosnia and Herzegovina may warrant a different approach. It is not clear that many of the state enterprises that are not servicing their loans still have any value as going concerns. Because of the war many enterprises are not functioning at all or are functioning at negligible levels of activity. In these cases attempts to resurrect the old company will not do much good and the alternative of simply selling off assets to the private sector is worth considering. If such a strategy is followed, the remaining loan obligations might as well be transferred to the settlement fund. Any revenue received from the asset sales could be allocated to the fund so as to contribute to at least a partial payment.

As was already mentioned, care should be taken, to avoid the possibility of a dominant ownership role by major borrowers. If such a situation already exists it could be changed by imposing proper loan classification procedures and applying capital adequacy ratios and other prudential regulations. This will, in most cases, effectively renationalize the bank, after which a sounder privatization strategy can be designed. Among other things, this approach would allow consolidation prior to sales, which is likely to be necessary.

Finally, as with all Eastern European banks, technical assistance is urgently needed. Management information systems, credit control procedures, credit assessment techniques, and the like are all in need of improvement. Twinning arrangements have been used successfully in many countries. While the size of Bosnia and Herzegovina and continuing uncertainty in the political sphere make it unlikely that such arrangements can be put in place in the near future, more limited forms of technical assistance could be devised.

Complications will arise if regional supervision agencies emerge. This development should be avoided if possible but may be necessary as a transitional arrangement. Care should be taken to coordinate regulatory policies, accounting standards, and information requirements.

V. MEDIUM-TERM PROSPECTS AND FINANCING REQUIREMENTS

An early and robust economic recovery will require effective implementation of sound macroeconomic policies, structural reforms, and a well-coordinated reconstruction program—important issues that are the focus of the previous sections. Clearly, such a program will require considerable external assistance. As described earlier, based on the joint efforts of the government, the World Bank, the EU, and other agencies, a reconstruction program requiring a minimum of $5.1 billion of external financing over the 1996-1998 period is being proposed to the donor community. However, Bosnia and Herzegovina also inherited a considerable amount of external debt, much of it now in arrears. Unless it addresses its foreign debt problems, Bosnia and Herzegovina will not be able to normalize its financial relations with creditors, official or private, thus inhibiting its ability to access the international financial resources that will be needed for longer-term growth. Resolving the debt problem is, therefore, a key issue for restoring sustainable growth.

Addressing the External Debt Problem

Bosnia and Herzegovina's total external debt at the end of 1995 amounted to $3.2 billion, of which $1.9 billion is in arrears (table 5.1). These debt figures represent the sum of Bosnia and Herzegovina's share of the former Yugoslavia's total long-term external debts, derived on the basis of final beneficiary principle for debts whose beneficiaries are identifiable, and its share of nonallocated debts, from former Yugoslavia, assigned by using Bosnia and Herzegovina's quota share of the former Yugoslavia's quota in the International Monetary Fund (IMF).

Bosnia and Herzegovina's current high and unsustainable debt indicators originate from the collapse of its economy over the past four years. GDP declined from more than $8-9 billion in 1990 to about $2.2 billion in 1995, and total exports (including those to other former Yugoslav republics) declined from $3 billion to less than $300 million. Debt indicators, using 1995 GDP and trade figures, therefore look very poor, with the country's ratio of debt to GDP at 147 percent and the ratio of required debt service to total exports around 130 percent. Clearly, Bosnia and Herzegovina is in no position to service such levels of debt obligations now or in the near future. The experiences of other countries with reconstruction in the aftermath of major conflicts strongly suggests that a quick resolution to debt problems such as those currently plaguing Bosnia and Herzegovina is imperative.

An effective solution would ideally have two characteristics. First, Bosnia and Herzegovina is in no position to make any net payments for several years to come. Thus *cash flow relief* is necessary to ensure a strongly positive net transfer into Bosnia and Herzegovina. Second, once foreign assistance declines, access to private capital markets needs to be secured to ensure continued recovery. At current levels of debt, such renewed access to private markets is out of the question; the current ratio of debt to GDP is more than twice as high as Mexico's before that country's Brady deal. Thus a debt restructuring would need to provide not only cash flow relief but would also, desirably, provide significant debt relief so as to bring the debt-output ratio back to serviceable levels. Without prejudging any final settlement that might be reached with the Paris and London Clubs, a comprehensive workout would clearly contribute significantly to creating the conditions needed to restore creditworthiness and to permit private sector inflows to make a contribution to the reconstruction effort in the outer years.

A serious problem is that a workout of senior debt alone (such as Paris Club debts), and ahead of restructuring other debts, often results in benefits for the junior creditors—in this case the commercial debt holders. The more debt relief from the Paris Club, the less the discount commercial banks are likely to offer, since the market value of their claims goes up with every dollar the senior debt gets reduced. Unless the Paris Club package is structured to avoid this outcome, the commercial banks, not Bosnia and Herzegovina, will be the main beneficiary of any Paris Club deal.

Table 5.1 Estimated total external debt by creditor; end-1995 (millions of U.S. dollars)		
Creditor	**Outstanding debt**	**In arrears**
Multilateral	709	471
IBRD	623	447
IMF	49	0
Other	37	24
Paris Club	571	486
London Club	1,112	384
Other creditors	842	600
Total	**3.234**	**1.941**

One way to deal with this problem is the Polish model, that is, to tranche the Paris Club package and make the second tranche conditional on there being an equally generous package from the London Club. In Poland, failure to match by commercial banks would not only have voided the second tranche, it also would have restored the debt restructured in the first tranche to its original terms. This is a very serious threat to the commercial banks because of the Paris Club creditors' seniority.

External Financing Requirements

Considerable external financing will be needed to normalize Bosnia and Herzegovina's relations with external creditors, as well as to cover the requirements of the reconstruction program. This normalization involves both the clearance of outstanding arrears as well as the restructuring and servicing of remaining debts. An important first step in this direction was already taken on December 20, 1995, with the clearance of outstanding arrears owed to the International Monetary Fund. On March 12, 1996, the World Bank's Board of Executive Directors also adopted a debt consolidation plan for Bosnia and Herzegovina that will clear its arrears to the Bank and reduce Bank-related debt service requirements in the immediate following years. Normalization of relations with other multilateral creditors is also expected to take place soon. A comprehensive debt workout would be desirable to normalize Bosnia's financial relations with other official and private creditors. The scenario presented in this section is illustrative, and it is in no way intended to prejudge the outcome of future negotiations with Bosnia's external creditors in the Paris and the London Clubs. It shows however that a comprehensive debt workout, including a substantial net present value reduction on consolidated debt service to Paris Club creditors and a substantial debt stock reduction with London Club creditors goes a long way to create the conditions necessary to re-establish Bosnia's creditworthiness for IBRD lending starting in 1998 and private capital inflows after 2000. Less generous terms would leave Bosnia's creditworthiness more fragile and access to such flows in question. Key elements of this illustrative scenario are as follows:

- Clearance of about $640 million in outstanding loans, including arrears due the World Bank in mid-1996, via their consolidation and refinancing into a new loan with 30 years maturity including a grace period of 5 years. The Bank also plans to support Bosnia with some $400 million of IDA resources over the next 2-3 years, over and above a special Bosnia and Herzegovina Trust Fund of $150 million already established by the Bank in January 1996 on a combination of grant and IDA terms. A net transfer of some $450 million from the World Bank Group is anticipated over the next 3-4 years.

- Clearance of arrears owed to other multilateral creditors in mid-1996.

- Clearance of pre-cutoff date arrears to Paris Club creditors in mid-1996, via "Naples terms", i.e. two-thirds net present value (NPV) reduction on consolidated debt service, and a deferral of post-cutoff date debt arrears over a 6 year period, including 3 years of grace.

- A 100 percent rollover of debt service on London Club and suppliers' debts for 1996-97, followed by a two-thirds debt stock reduction at Naples terms, in 1998, and rescheduling of the remaining London Club and suppliers' debt over 23 years, with 6 years grace period.

Under this scenario, Bosnia and Herzegovina's gross external financing requirements will total about $12.7 billion over the period 1996-2000 (table 5.2, line I). The lion's share ($7.6 billion, line I.1) of this five-year financing requirement comes from the current account deficit, largely driven by reconstruction needs, and to a lesser extent from other import requirements (humanitarian imports and private sector imports). The next largest financing requirement ($2.7 billion, line I.4) is accounted for by arrears clearance. Debt service on rescheduled and new debt to multilateral and Paris Club creditors accounts for about $1 billion (line I.2), or 8 percent of the financing requirement. Debt service to London Club and other commercial creditors, including rollover of debt service in 1996-1997, accounts for 0.9 billion (line I.3), or 7 percent of the financing requirement, and the accumulation of international reserves to a minimum precautionary level for about $0.5 billion (line I.5), or 4 percent.

These gross financing requirements are projected to be met through a combination of sources. About $2.1 billion (line II.1) of the total financing (16 percent) is assumed to be provided through official and private unrequited transfers. Official unrequited transfers are assumed to decline over time as humanitarian assistance is replaced by reconstruction assistance on concessional terms (line II.1a). Private unrequited transfers (line II.1b) are also expected to decline gradually over time, mainly reflecting the combined evaluation of its two components: emergency assistance needs that are currently addressed by nongovernmental organizations, which are assumed to decline over time, and private remittances from Bosnian families working abroad, which are are assumed to remain constant over the projection period. Foreign direct investment inflows are expected to resume starting in 1998 and provide about $ 0.5 billion financing (line II.3).

New cash financing (about $5.1 billion; line II.2) by various creditors in support of the reconstruction and recovery program would cover forty percent of the total financing requirement, most of it on concessional terms. In addition, multilateral creditors, bilateral creditors (including Paris Club creditors), and commercial creditors (including London Club creditors) are expected to finance about eighty percent of the remaining $5 billion financing gap (line III) via arrears clearance. The World Bank adjustment lending in support of the economic reform program would provide additional financing of about $0.2 billion.[5] The remaining financing gap for the 5 year period is close to $1 billion (line III.3), averaging about $190 million a year, or 7 percent of the total financing requirements. It bears repeating, however, that this calculation of the remaining financing gap *assumes that financing for the*

---

[5]   The proposed World Bank adjustment credits are expected to be cofinanced by other creditors. This cofinancing from other creditors will contribute to filling the financing gap.

Table 5.2 External financing requirements, 1995-2000[a]
(millions of U.S. dollars)

	1995	1996	1997	1998	1999	2000	96-2000
I. Financing needs	*1,336*	*3,276*	*2,629*	*4,072*	*1,800*	*993*	*12,770*
1. Current account deficit excluding interest and transfers	751	1,561	2,085	1,949	1,395	628	7,618
2. Debt service to multilateral and Paris Club creditors	256	311	148	149	190	185	983
a. On existing debt	256	252	76	69	82	77	556
b. On new debt	0	59	72	80	108	108	427
3. Debt service to London Club and other commercial creditors[b]	249	243	246	160	165	130	944
4. Arrears clearance[c]	38	1,011	0	1724	0	0	2,735
5. Change in gross reserves (+:increase)	42	150	150	90	50	50	490
II. Financing sources	*1,336*	*1,630*	*2,118*	*1,921*	*1,383*	*673*	*7,725*
1. Unrequited net transfers	737	830	468	371	253	223	2,145
a. Official	343	422	265	193	100	70	1,050
b. Private	394	408	203	178	153	153	1,095
2. New financing for reconstruction[d]	0	800	1,650	1,450	930	250	5,080
a. Official transfers for reconstruction	0	560	1,155	1,015	651	175	3,556
b. New medium and long term capital inflows	0	240	495	435	279	75	1,524
3. Foreign direct investment	0	0	0	100	200	200	500
5. Exceptional financing	505	0	0	0	0	0	0
6. Others[e]	94	0	0	0	0	0	0
III. Financing gap	*0*	*1,647*	*511*	*2,151*	*417*	*320*	*5,048*
1. Arrears clearance and debt relief	0	1,392	246	1,915	199	167	3,919
a. World Bank arrears clearance plan	0	639	0	0	0	0	639
b. Rollover/debt relief, London Club and other commercial creditors	0	243	246	1,915	199	167	2,770
c. Clearance of arrears to Paris Club	0	486	0	0	0	0	486
d. Clearance of arrears to other multilateral creditors	0	24	0	0	0	0	24
2. World Bank adjustment lending[f]	0	90	35	30	30	0	185
3a. Remaining financing gap[g]	0	165	230	207	188	154	944
b. (Before clearance of arrears to Paris Club and other multilateral creditors.)	0	675	230	207	188	154	1,454
IV. Memo items							
1. Total external debt/GDP (%)	147	123	119	72	70	67	83
2. Debt service/Total exports (%)[h]	130	51	33	12	14	12	24

a. 1995 is estimated; 1996-2000 are projected.

b. Assumes rollover of debt service in 1996 and 1997 and debt service at terms comparable with Naples terms thereafter, (including late interest).

c. Assumes clearance of arrears to multilateral creditors including IBRD and Paris Club in mid-1996, and to London Club and other commercial creditors in 1998.

d. Assumes that financing of reconstruction program is fully secured.

e. Includes use of IMF resources ($45 million), errors and omissions.

f. Assumes that the first proposed World Bank structural adjustment credit to Bosnia and Herzegovina, which is currently under preparation, will be disbursed in 1996. The World Bank lending program includes two more proposed structural adjustment credits, amounting to $95 million, to be disbursed over 1997-98. Of course, any World Bank adjustment lending would be conditional on an acceptable macroeconomic program, supported and agreed jointly with the IMF.

g. After clearance of arrears to multilateral creditors, Paris Club, London Club and other commercial creditors, but before balance of payment financing from IMF, multilateral creditors other than the Bank, and bilateral creditors.

h. 1995 figure refers to scheduled debt service.

Note: The Bank scenario is illustrative, and it in no way is intended to prejudge the outcome of future negotiations with Bosnia's external creditors in the Paris and the London Clubs. It shows that a comprehensive debt workout including a substantial net present value reduction on the consolidated service with Paris Club creditors and a substantial debt stock reduction with London Club creditors goes a long way to create the conditions necessary for renewal of IBRD lending starting in 1998 and private capital inflows after 2000.

Source: Data provided by Bosnia and Herzegovina authorities, the IMF, and World Bank staff estimates.

reconstruction program has already been fully secured and, that a comprehensive debt workout will have contributed to substantial debt relief as mentioned above. This remaining financing gap would be covered by balance of payments support from the IMF, multilateral creditors other than the Bank, and bilateral creditors

This debt workout scenario illustrates the contribution that both debt service relief and debt stock reduction can make to the restoration of creditworthiness. Under the scenario, the overall debt parameters would indicate a substantial decline in debt and debt service indicators. For example, the ratio of debt to GDP would fall from 147 percent in 1995 to about 67 percent by 2000, and the composition of debt stock will be more favorable in terms of the degree of concessionality of the debt terms implied by the remaining debt stock. With such a strategy, it is possible that a viable medium-term economic program, based on restoration of country creditworthiness and renewed access to international commercial capital markets, can be realistically envisaged and sustained growth be expected. Less generous terms would leave Bosnia's creditworthiness more fragile.

The Macroeconomic Outlook

Given the uncertainty and complexity of implementing this program in the immediate postwar environment, forecasting the growth outlook is at best a highly tentative exercise. The scenario presented here is, therefore, only illustrative (table 5.3). It assumes that substantial reconstruction financing on concessional terms and debt relief will be provided by multilateral and bilateral creditors; that considerable discipline will be maintained in domestic policies for the effective use of external assistance and effective implementation of the economic reform program; that public sector institutional reforms will proceed well; and that conditions that allow for a rise in long-term private flows will be in place by the year 2000.

Should these conditions prevail, Bosnia and Herzegovina's economy could start to rebound strongly. Given the extreme deterioration of public services and infrastructure facilities resulting from the war, the initial impetus for growth will clearly come from aid-supported reconstruction efforts for at least the next couple of years: transport, communications, energy supply, and other infrastructure need to be repaired and hundreds of thousands of refugees and displaced persons need to be resettled and soldiers demobilized, with attendant housing and employment needs. Private investment is also expected to recover given the urgent needs for repair and extension of existing businesses and housing. Assuming that long-term finance will be available, private investment will rebound most likely in light industry, services (mainly transport, tourism, and financial institutions) and housing construction. The capital requirements of these investments are relatively small and their dependence on public infrastructure and services is limited. The agricultural sector, dominated by private smallholders, could also be a candidate for early recovery if food aid is managed so that it avoids a negative impact on domestic producers. It will take somewhat longer for trade to return to its prewar export levels. Until basic infrastructure is rehabilitated

					Ave.	Ave.
Table 5.3[a] **Selected economic indicators, 1991-2005** **(millions of U.S. dollars)**						
	1991	**1994**	**1995**	**1996**	**1996-00**	**2001-05**
I. Gross Domestic Product (GDP)						
1. GDP (US$ million)	8,199	na	2,200	3,100	4,840	8,900
2. Real GDP growth (%)	na	na	na	35	21	8.4
3. Per capita income (U.S. dollars)	1,872	na	524	728	1,150	2,123
II. External Trade Account						
1. Merchandise exports (US$ million)	2,120	164	295	608	1,230	2,447
2. Real merchandise export growth (%)	na	na	77	100	43	6
3. Share of merchandise exports in GDP (%)	34	na	13	20	25	27
4. Merchandise imports (US$ million)	1,673	889	759	1,722	2,384	2,779
a. Reconstruction related	0	0	0	612	780	0
b. Humanitarian and in-kind aid	0	498	203	297	89	0
c. Other	1,673	391	556	813	1,544	2,779
5. Real merchandise import growth (%)	na	na	na	120	29	7
6. Share of merchandise imports in GDP (%)	33	na	35	56	51	31
(Reconstruction related and other imports- excluding humanitarian imports)	na	na	25	46	48	31
7. Trade balance (in % of GDP)	5	na	-21	-36	-25	-4
III. External Current Account						
1. Current account balance (in % of GDP)	na	na	na	-32	-30	-4
(Excluding official transfers)	na	na	na	-45	-35	-5
IV. International Reserves						
1. Total reserves (in months of imports)	na	na	0.4	1.2	1.9	3.0
(in months of reconstruction related and other imports-excluding humanitarian)	na	na	0.5	1.5	1.9	3.0

a. 1991-95 are estimated; 1996-2005 are projected.

na: not available

Note: The Bank scenario is illustrative, and it in no way is intended to prejudge the outcome of future negotiations with Bosnia's external creditors in the Paris and London Clubs. It shows that a comprehensive debt workout including a substantial net present value reduction on consolidated debt service with Paris Club creditors and a substantial debt stock reduction with London Club creditors goes a long way to create the conditions necessary for renewal of IBRD lending starting in 1998 and private capital inflows after 2000, and for achievement of a sustainable growth.

Source: Data provided by Bosnia and Herzegovina authorities, the IMF, and World Bank estimates.

and public services are restored, exports are not likely to constitute a significant source of growth.

Experience from other countries similarly afflicted by war suggests that a strong reconstruction and recovery program could help Bosnia and Herzegovina's economy rebound significantly, by around 35-40 percent in 1996 and at progressively declining rates thereafter (table 5.3, line I.2). This, however, requires good progress on the ground in government institution-building, sound policies, and effective coordination among parties. However, even under this scenario, GDP would only reach close to two-thirds of its prewar level by 2000. The prewar level of GDP would be recovered in 7-9 years.

As the economy recovers and domestic supply capacity is restored, some of the prewar export markets are expected to be regained, and exports are projected to recover from their current low base to about two-thirds of their prewar levels by 2000. Beyond the reconstruction phase, with significant recovery and freer access to inputs, labor, and capital, normal trade patterns are projected to resume, leading to a large improvement in the trade balance. Based on these assumptions, the average trade deficit is projected to decline from about 24 percent of GDP during 1996-2000 to 4 percent in 2001-05 (line II.7).

It should be underlined once again that if the conditions underlying the above scenario were not in place, resulting inter alia from a significant shortfall in donor financing for the reconstruction program, policy slippages in implementation of stabilization and economic reform programs, and/or unfavorable debt workouts with London and Paris Club creditors, the scenario illustrated here would not be achieved. Such a development would undoubtedly put at risk the possibility of lasting peace and prosperity in Bosnia and Herzegovina.

Distributors of World Bank Publications

Prices and credit terms vary from country to country. Consult your local distributor before placing an order.

ALBANIA
Adrion Ltd.
Perlat Rexhepi Str.
Pall 9, Shk. 1, Ap. 4
Tirana
Tel: (42) 274 19; 221 72
Fax: (42) 274 19

ARGENTINA
Oficina del Libro Internacional
Av. Cordoba 1877
1120 Buenos Aires
Tel: (1) 815-8156
Fax: (1) 815-8354

AUSTRALIA, FIJI, PAPUA NEW GUINEA, SOLOMON ISLANDS, VANUATU, AND WESTERN SAMOA
D.A. Information Services
648 Whitehorse Road
Mitcham 3132
Victoria
Tel: (61) 3 9210 7777
Fax: (61) 3 9210 7788
URL: http://www.dadirect.com.au

AUSTRIA
Gerold and Co.
Graben 31
A-1011 Wien
Tel: (1) 533-50-14-0
Fax: (1) 512-47-31-29

BANGLADESH
Micro Industries Development
Assistance Society (MIDAS)
House 5, Road 16
Dhanmondi R/Area
Dhaka 1209
Tel: (2) 326427
Fax: (2) 811188

BELGIUM
Jean De Lannoy
Av. du Roi 202
1060 Brussels
Tel: (2) 538-5169
Fax: (2) 538-0841

BRAZIL
Publicações Tecnicas Internacionais Ltda.
Rua Peixoto Gomide, 209
01409 Sao Paulo, SP.
Tel: (11) 259-6644
Fax: (11) 258-6990

CANADA
Renouf Publishing Co. Ltd.
1294 Algoma Road
Ottawa, Ontario K1B 3W8
Tel: 613-741-4333
Fax: 613-741-5439

CHINA
China Financial & Economic
Publishing House
8, Da Fo Si Dong Jie
Beijing
Tel: (1) 333-8257
Fax: (1) 401-7365

COLOMBIA
Infoenlace Ltda.
Apartado Aereo 34270
Bogota D.E.
Tel: (1) 285-2798
Fax: (1) 285-2798

COTE D'IVOIRE
Centre d'Edition et de Diffusion
Africaines (CEDA)
04 B.P. 541
Abidjan 04 Plateau
Tel: 225-24-6510
Fax: 225-25-0567

CYPRUS
Center of Applied Research
Cyprus College
6, Diogenes Street, Engomi
P.O. Box 2006
Nicosia
Tel: 244-1730
Fax: 246-2051

CZECH REPUBLIC
National Information Center
prodejna, Konviktska 5
CS – 113 57 Prague 1
Tel: (2) 2422-9433
Fax: (2) 2422-1484
URL: http://www.nis.cz/

DENMARK
SamfundsLitteratur
Rosenoerns Allé 11
DK-1970 Frederiksberg C
Tel: (31)-351942
Fax: (31)-357822

ECUADOR
Facultad Latinoamericana de
Ciencias Sociales
FLASCO-SEDE Ecuador
Calle Ulpiano Paez 118
y Av. Patria
Quito, Ecuador
Tel/Fax: (2) 542 714; 542 716; 528 200
Fax: (2) 566 139

EGYPT, ARAB REPUBLIC OF
Al Ahram
Al Galaa Street
Cairo
Tel: (2) 578-6083
Fax: (2) 578-6833

The Middle East Observer
41, Sherif Street
Cairo
Tel: (2) 393-9732
Fax: (2) 393-9732

FINLAND
Akateeminen Kirjakauppa
P.O. Box 23
FIN-00371 Helsinki
Tel: (0) 12141
Fax: (0) 121-4441
URL: http://booknet.cultnet.fi/aka/

FRANCE
World Bank Publications
66, avenue d'Iéna
75116 Paris
Tel: (1) 40-69-30-56/57
Fax: (1) 40-69-30-68

GERMANY
UNO-Verlag
Poppelsdorfer Allee 55
53115 Bonn
Tel: (228) 212940
Fax: (228) 217492

GREECE
Papasotiriou S.A.
35, Stournara Str.
106 82 Athens
Tel: (1) 364-1826
Fax: (1) 364-8254

HONG KONG, MACAO
Asia 2000 Ltd.
Sales & Circulation Department
Seabird House, unit 1101-02
22-28 Wyndham Street, Central
Hong Kong
Tel: 852 2530-1409
Fax: 852 2526-1107
URL: http://www.sales@asia2000.com.hk

HUNGARY
Foundation for Market
Economy
Dombovari Ut 17-19
H-1117 Budapest
Tel: 36 1 204 2951 or
36 1 204 2948
Fax: 36 1 204 2953

INDIA
Allied Publishers Ltd.
751 Mount Road
Madras - 600 002
Tel: (44) 852-3938
Fax: (44) 852-0649

INDONESIA
Pt. Indira Limited
Jalan Borobudur 20
P.O. Box 181
Jakarta 10320
Tel: (21) 390-4290
Fax: (21) 421-4289

IRAN
Kowkab Publishers
P.O. Box 19575-511
Tehran
Tel: (21) 258-3723
Fax: 98 (21) 258-3723

Ketab Sara Co. Publishers
Khaled Eslamboli Ave.,
6th Street
Kushel Delafrooz No. 8
Tehran
Tel: 8717819 or 8716104
Fax: 8862479

IRELAND
Government Supplies Agency
Oifig an tSoláthair
4-5 Harcourt Road
Dublin 2
Tel: (1) 461-3111
Fax: (1) 475-2670

ISRAEL
Yozmot Literature Ltd.
P.O. Box 56055
Tel Aviv 61560
Tel: (3) 5285-397
Fax: (3) 5285-397

R.O.Y. International
PO Box 13056
Tel Aviv 61130
Tel: (3) 5461423
Fax: (3) 5461442

Palestinian Authority/Middle East
Index Information Services
P.O.B. 19502 Jerusalem
Tel: (2) 271219

ITALY
Licosa Commissionaria Sansoni SPA
Via Duca Di Calabria, 1/1
Casella Postale 552
50125 Firenze
Tel: (55) 645-415
Fax: (55) 641-257

JAMAICA
Ian Randle Publishers Ltd.
206 Old Hope Road
Kingston 6
Tel: 809-927-2085
Fax: 809-977-0243

JAPAN
Eastern Book Service
Hongo 3-Chome,
Bunkyo-ku 113
Tokyo
Tel: (03) 3818-0861
Fax: (03) 3818-0864
URL: http://www.bekkoame.or.jp/~svt-ebs

KENYA
Africa Book Service (E.A.) Ltd.
Quaran House, Mfangano Street
P.O. Box 45245
Nairobi
Tel: (2) 23641
Fax: (2) 330272

KOREA, REPUBLIC OF
Daejon Trading Co. Ltd.
P.O. Box 34
Yeoeida
Seoul
Tel: (2) 785-1631/4
Fax: (2) 784-0315

MALAYSIA
University of Malaya Cooperative
Bookshop, Limited
P.O. Box 1127
Jalan Pantai Baru
59700 Kuala Lumpur
Tel: (3) 756-5000
Fax: (3) 755-4424

MEXICO
INFOTEC
Apartado Postal 22-860
14060 Tlalpan,
Mexico D.F.
Tel: (5) 606-0011
Fax: (5) 606-0386

NETHERLANDS
De Lindeboom/InOr-Publikaties
P.O. Box 202
7480 AE Haaksbergen
Tel: (53) 574-0004
Fax: (53) 572-9296

NEW ZEALAND
Private Mail Bag 99914
New Market
Auckland
Tel: (9) 524-8119
Fax: (9) 524-8067

NIGERIA
University Press Limited
Three Crowns Building Jericho
Private Mail Bag 5095
Ibadan
Tel: (22) 41-1356
Fax: (22) 41-2056

NORWAY
Narvesen Information Center
Book Department
P.O. Box 6125 Etterstad
N-0602 Oslo 6
Tel: (22) 57-3300
Fax: (22) 68-1901

PAKISTAN
Mirza Book Agency
65, Shahrah-e-Quaid-e-Azam
P.O. Box No. 729
Lahore 54000
Tel: (42) 7353601
Fax: (42) 7585283

Oxford University Press
5 Bangalore Town
Sharae Faisal
PO Box 13033
Karachi-75350
Tel: (21) 446307
Fax: (21) 454-7640

PERU
Editorial Desarrollo SA
Apartado 3824
Lima 1
Tel: (14) 285380
Fax: (14) 286628

PHILIPPINES
International Booksource Center Inc.
Suite 720, Cityland 10
Condominium Tower 2
H.V dela Costa, corner
Valero St.
Makati, Metro Manila
Tel: (2) 817-9676
Fax: (2) 817-1741

POLAND
International Publishing Service
Ul. Piekna 31/37
00-577 Warzawa
Tel: (2) 628-6089
Fax: (2) 621-7255

PORTUGAL
Livraria Portugal
Rua Do Carmo 70-74
1200 Lisbon
Tel: (1) 347-4982
Fax: (1) 347-0264

ROMANIA
Compani De Librarii Bucuresti S.A.
Str. Lipscani no. 26, sector 3
Bucharest
Tel: (1) 613 9645
Fax: (1) 312 4000

RUSSIAN FEDERATION
Isdatelstvo <Ves Mir>
9a, Kolpachniy Pereulok
Moscow 101831
Tel: (95) 917 87 49
Fax: (95) 917 92 59

SAUDI ARABIA, QATAR
Jarir Book Store
P.O. Box 3196
Riyadh 11471
Tel: (1) 477-3140
Fax: (1) 477-2940

SINGAPORE, TAIWAN, MYANMAR, BRUNEI
Asahgate Publishing Asia
Pacific Pte. Ltd.
41 Kallang Pudding Road #04-03
Golden Wheel Building
Singapore 349316
Tel: (65) 741-5166
Fax: (65) 742-9356
e-mail: ashgate@asianconnect.com

SLOVAK REPUBLIC
Slovart G.T.G. Ltd.
Krupinska 4
PO Box 152
852 99 Bratislava 5
Tel: (7) 839472
Fax: (7) 839485

SOUTH AFRICA, BOTSWANA
For single titles:
Oxford University Press
Southern Africa
P.O. Box 1141
Cape Town 8000
Tel: (21) 45-7266
Fax: (21) 45-7265

For subscription orders:
International Subscription Service
P.O. Box 41095
Craighall
Johannesburg 2024
Tel: (11) 880-1448
Fax: (11) 880-6248

SPAIN
Mundi-Prensa Libros, S.A.
Castello 37
28001 Madrid
Tel: (1) 431-3399
Fax: (1) 575-3998
http://www.tsai.es/mprensa

Mundi-Prensa Barcelona
Consell de Cent, 391
08009 Barcelona
Tel: (3) 488-3009
Fax: (3) 487-7659

SRI LANKA, THE MALDIVES
Lake House Bookshop
P.O. Box 244
100, Sir Chittampalam A.
Gardiner Mawatha
Colombo 2
Tel: (1) 32105
Fax: (1) 432104

SWEDEN
Fritzes Customer Service
Regeringsgaton 12
S-106 47 Stockholm
Tel: (8) 690 90 90
Fax: (8) 21 4777

Wennergren-Williams AB
P.O. Box 1305
S-171 25 Solna
Tel: (8) 705-97-50
Fax: (8) 27-00-71

SWITZERLAND
Librairie Payot
Service Institutionnel
Côtes-de-Montbenon 30
1002 Lausanne
Tel: (021)-320-2511
Fax: (021)-311-1393

Van Diermen Editions Techniq
Ch. de Lacuez 41
CH1807 Blonay
Tel: (021) 943 2673
Fax: (021) 943 3605

TANZANIA
Oxford University Press
Maktaba Street
PO Box 5299
Dar es Salaam
Tel: (51) 29209
Fax: (51) 46822

THAILAND
Central Books Distribution
306 Silom Road
Bangkok
Tel: (2) 235-5400
Fax: (2) 237-8321

TRINIDAD & TOBAGO, JAM.
Systematics Studies Unit
#9 Watts Street
Curepe
Trinidad, West Indies
Tel: 809-662-5654
Fax: 809-662-5654

UGANDA
Gustro Ltd.
Madhvani Building
Plot 16/4 Jinja Rd.
Kampala
Tel/Fax: (41) 254763

UNITED KINGDOM
Microinfo Ltd.
P.O. Box 3
Alton, Hampshire GU34 2PG
England
Tel: (1420) 86848
Fax: (1420) 89889

ZAMBIA
University Bookshop
Great East Road Campus
P.O. Box 32379
Lusaka
Tel: (1) 213221 Ext. 482

ZIMBABWE
Longman Zimbabwe (Pte.)Ltd
Tourle Road, Ardbennie
P.O. Box ST125
Southerton
Harare
Tel: (4) 662711
Fax: (4) 662716